Debbie Ross

organic
strong
wholemeal
bread flour

100% whole
cookery and

DOVES FARM

DOVES FARM
· EST · 1978 ·

ORGANIC
Stoneground from whole grain
this 100% rye flour is naturally
low in gluten, producing close
textured bread and cakes with a
pleasing continental flavour.

WHOLEMEAL

Rye flour

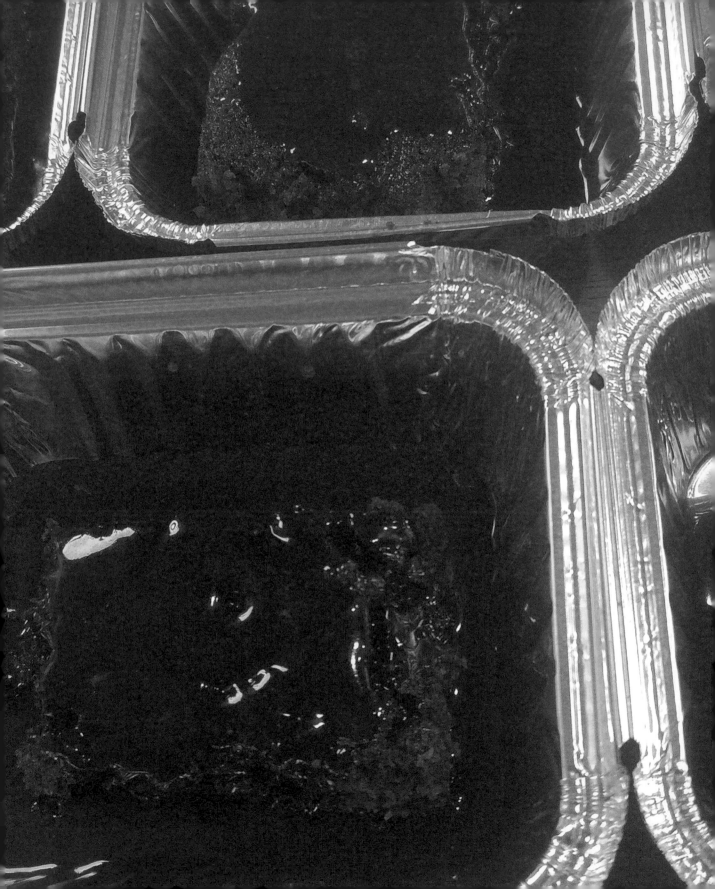

Highland HOME COOK

the cook book

Debbie Ross

Ross
Cottage
Publishing

Dedication

This book is dedicated to my Mum, who made home-cooked food pretty much every day throughout my childhood.

ISBN 978-1-9161556-0-2

First published in the UK in 2019 by Ross Cottage Publishing

Printed in Scotland by J Thomson
https://www.jtcp.co.uk/

Errata

Any errors found in this book after it was published will be corrected in the next edition. In the meatime, errors and their corrections can be found here:

highlandhomecook.co.uk/rcp

Ross Cottage Publishing

Contents

Thanks

About the Author

Debbie Ross is HHC. At age 8, she put a pinny on and has never taken it off. A prolific recipe writer, her creations have appeared, occasionally, in magazines, on her blog, and now for the first time, in her own cookbook.

She was a finalist in the first Hampshire Fare Cookery Competition - a home cook up against two professional chefs - and once cooked, and danced, on stage at the BBC Good Food Show with Ainsley Harriet.

She lives with her husband, in the Highlands of Scotland, in a cottage at the top of a hill overlooking the Cromarty Firth.

She turned her lifelong love of cooking into a career in 2015 and you can find her with her bread and bakes at markets and food events across the Highlands.

Introduction

It is strange that I earn a crust - pun intended - from making bread and cooking. As a youngster, I wasn't a very confident cook. My Mum spent a lot of time in hospital when I was a child and there was no Granny to bake cakes with. When Mum was around, she cooked from scratch daily and so a certain amount of learning came about through a sort of osmosis.

My first efforts at baking were inedible; the litmus test - our Labrador - who would eat pretty much anything. The rock hard biscuits remained untouched. Later attempts at cooking included roast chicken, accompanied by the giblets still inside the bird in their plastic bag - not a great success either.

Cooking was compulsory for the first two years of senior school and my cookery teacher, who shall remain nameless, told me I was useless and would never be able to make pastry after a failed attempt at apple pie. Thankfully, I was outraged rather than defeated and persuaded a family friend to give me lessons until I could make pastry competently. I gave up formal cookery lessons as soon as I could!

Around the same time, I become a vegetarian, much to my family's consternation; yet it was here that my food journey really began. I cooked my way through Constance Spry and Delia Smith, meat dishes included, although I never ate them! When Sara Brown's *Vegetarian Kitchen* came out in the 80's, I was smitten and cooked and ate my way through that too.

Cooking confidence, like anything else, increases with practice and I was soon conjuring up meat-free meals, learning about diet and nutrition, and eventually, in my 30's, qualifying as a professional cook.

Whatever your food journey and current preferences, I hope this cookbook will increase your confidence and joy in preparing and eating food.

For more information, please visit my website and my blog, or connect with me on social media:

HHC web: highlandhomecook.co.uk   **Blog:** highlandhomecook.co.uk/scrapingthebowl

 facebook.com/highlandhomecook   twitter.com/highlandcook

A Note on my Food Philosophy

I'm not going to lecture you. You didn't buy this book for me to ram my food philosophy down your throat. If you want to know more about my philosophy and about seasonal eating, check out my website here:

http://www.highlandhomecook.co.uk/philosophy

At the end of the day, we genuinely are what we eat, so it makes sense to care about what we consume. For personal reasons, I eat mostly organic and, where possible, homegrown and local food. If you are lucky enough to have local independent food suppliers, you might consider giving them a try. Buying food that has the least 'food miles', for where you are, means you'll be helping to reduce carbon emissions from transportation. The closer to home you can find your food, the fresher it is likely to be too.

I'm not decrying supermarkets. Most of us have no choice about where we buy our food and have limited budgets, so buy as fresh as you can, be it a market, farm shop or supermarket. Frozen veg are a good choice if you're on a low income, or even if you're not, as they are relatively cheap, can be found all year round, and the nutrition is often well preserved.

I only buy organic free-range eggs. Anything else is from caged hens or hens 'with access to open pasture' who have been fed genetically modified (GM) grain. If you have a small local supplier check how the hens have been reared and what they eat, then make your own choices.

The Highland Home Cook Store Cupboard

I was never deprived of food as a child, although looking at my store cupboard, you wouldn't think so. I'm a food hoarder. Even before I was cooking for a living, I kept huge quantities of dried goods and a cupboard full of tins. I'm not suggesting you need to do the same, absolutely not. I'm giving you a peek into my store cupboard so you can see what sort of ingredients you might want to have on hand if you're planning to cook these recipes, and to spare you rushing to the shops all the time. My nearest supermarket is a 30 mile round trip, so it pays for me to have a decent store of everyday food stuffs that keep well.

These are the tinned, jarred and bottled items I have on hand:
Italian tomatoes
Pulses, such as chickpeas
Olives
Capers
Artichokes
Coconut milk
Tinned fish
Sun-dried tomatoes

I also have a well-stocked dried-goods larder which includes:
Various types of pasta
Brown Basmati rice
Barley
Porridge oats
Polenta grain
Dried mushrooms
Sun-dried tomatoes
Dried herbs and spices including thyme, rosemary, sage, paprika, chilli, celery seeds, cumin, coriander, fennel, mixed spice
Dried beans, lentils and pulses including:
Red lentils
Puy lentils
Chickpeas
Butterbeans
Black beans
Pinto beans
A selection of dried fruits
Various flours, including strong flours for bread. You need to be using these routinely as the oils in wholemeal flours, in particular, oxidise and best before dates should be observed.

Other things I always have in are:
Grainy and Dijon mustard, Worcestershire sauce, cyder vinegar, yeast extract, tomato paste, miso paste, vegetable bouillon, dried yeast and honey.
I keep a range of oils, including coconut oil, and would expect you to have the oil or fat of your choice available to use for recipes.

A note on dried pulses
I buy my lentils, beans and pulses in bulk and store them in airtight containers, as I find this represents the best value. It also means you can take advantage of local plastic-free suppliers, where you can take your own containers and fill up with the amount of dried goods you require.

If you don't have the space for storing such items, or don't have the time to soak and cook them, tinned pulses work fine in most of the recipes.

Lentils don't require soaking and keeping a few hundred grams of a couple of types in your store cupboard is always worthwhile.

I keep nuts and seeds too, but unless you use these regularly it's best to buy them fresh, as the oils in them go rancid relatively quickly. Use best before dates as a guide.

A note on fresh herbs
Whilst not strictly a "store cupboard item", I always have fresh herbs to hand as I'm lucky enough to have a herb-garden outside my back door.

If you don't have space for herbs in your garden, you can always keep a few plants like parsley and basil on a sunny windowsill indoors.

A Note on Equipment

There's not much you really need to get started with any of these recipes. If you already cook, you'll probably already have everything you need in your kitchen cupboards.

If you're new to cooking, or don't have many utensils, these are the following items I would recommend as essential:

A digital scale - essential when weighing ingredients for bread and cakes in particular;

Graded measuring spoons - ¼ teaspoon to a tablespoon make measuring more precise;

A good chef's knife with a decent sized blade - you can't 'buy and try' and this can be an expensive bit of kit, so get the best you can afford to buy. It will last you if it's well looked after, so don't put it in the dishwasher.

A chef's steel - this will keep your knife sharp. Look at online videos on how to sharpen knives;

A heavy-based frying pan or skillet - a good one will set you back a bit, so save for the best you can afford and it will last you. If you can only afford one pan, buy a heavy-duty, non-stick so you can cook breads and pancakes in it without the need to buy a specialist item. Don't buy a cheap non-stick pan. It's never worth it.

A pan large enough for a family soup (1.5L), and a smaller pan for sauces (e.g. a milk pan). Buy the best you can afford as they'll last longer;

Mixing bowls of various sizes - If you don't want the expense of buying a load of bowls, a new and washed plastic washing-up bowl would do;

Decent sized chopping board;

Steel grater;

Rolling pin;

Oven-proof dish;

Selection of cake and bread tins and a heavy-duty baking sheet.

The only other piece of equipment I use routinely is a food processor, and some of the recipes do use one. However, if your kitchen doesn't have room, or you don't want to run to the expense, a good hand-held stick blender or mini food-chopper will tackle most of the jobs.

Oven Temperature Guide

This is a guide. All ovens vary. The best way to accurately tell the temperature in your own oven is to use an oven thermometer.

You will get to know your own oven, its hot-spots and quirks of cooking. There is no substitute for this experience and no recipe can be 100% accurate about cooking times. Use your senses and your experience and you won't go far wrong.

Descriptor	Electric °C	Electric (Fan) °C	Gas Mark
Very cool	110	90	¼
	120	100	½
Cool	140	120	1
	150	130	2
Moderate	160	140	3
	180	160	4
Moderately hot	190	170	5
	200	180	6
Hot	220	200	7
	230	210	8
Very hot	240	220	9

A Note on The Recipes

Some of the recipes, such as the ultimate chili con carne, vegetable chilli and the double chocolate brownies, are Highland Home Cook classics; others, inventions of necessity from my early days experimenting with veggie food. This isn't a vegetarian cookbook, although it certainly has a focus on vegetables. There's nothing fancy here, although I do promise you everything is tasty. I hope you will enjoy working your way through the book and discovering new things you can add to your own cooking repertoire. I encourage your feedback via my social media feeds or email.

Measures are in metric, for ease and accuracy. Most recipes will serve four people or more, a few are intended for two, and are clearly marked. Most ingredients you will have in your store cupboard or easily find in markets and supermarkets up and down the country. Anything that may be slightly unusual, I have suggested alternatives for.

Cooking times will depend on many things including your skill level and your oven type. The timings quoted are a rough guide.

All recipes assume you have olive oil to cook with - it's not included in the ingredients.

All the photographs in the book have been taken by me or my husband. They show REAL food cooked in a home kitchen and your results should turn out similar.

All recipes are double tested so you can cook them with the confidence that they will turn out well if you follow the instructions.

Happy Highland Home Cook cooking!

Recipe key:

 Suggestion of how many servings a recipe is likely to provide

 Estimated time this recipe will take to complete (not including any overnight components)

 This recipe is Vegetarian

 The resulting food from this recipe can be frozen (follow the instructions given)

 This recipe is Gluten-Free

 This recipe has an overnight component of some kind

Breakfasts and Brunches

Not enough cookbooks, in my view, contain breakfast recipes.

Cereal, toast and a cooked breakfast 'treat' may be all that most of us attempt, year in, year out. I think it's time to shake it up!

Commercial breakfast cereals are largely sugary and uninteresting, although millions of pounds are spent persuading us otherwise. Mostly big business succeeds.

I'm hoping this section will give you a few more interesting breakfasts to add to your armoury when you need some morning sustenance.

This is a tasty and filling dish which I turn to when inspiration is lacking. It barely needs a recipe. Its simplicity belies its flavour. Use this as the basis for your own savoury mushroom creations and you'll have a simple, quick and tasty breakfast up your sleeve.

Ingredients

4 large flat mushrooms such as Portabello
1 shallot - or half a small onion - very finely diced
1 garlic clove crushed
6 tbsp fresh breadcrumbs (by all means use dried breadcrumbs, but you will need less) or a couple of slices of bread, crusts removed, blitzed in a mini processor, or grated.
2 tsp fresh mixed herbs (rosemary, thyme)
seasoning to taste
30g strong cheese, I often use a Parmesan style cheese

Method

Remove the stalks from the mushrooms, leaving the gills intact. Finely chop the stalks.

Fry the diced shallot – or onion – until soft then add the chopped mushroom stalks and crushed garlic.

Place the breadcrumbs in a bowl and add the fried shallots – or onion – mushroom stalks, garlic and herbs. Season to taste.

Divide the mixture evenly between the mushrooms.

Grease a baking tray with oil or fat of your choice and place the mushrooms, stuffing side up, on the tray.

Drizzle with a little oil and top with the grated cheese. Bake until cooked and browning on top, 20 mins 190C/170C Fan/Gas 5.

I often serve this with eggs.

Proper Baked Beans on Toast

Who needs a recipe for this, right? Open tin, heat beans, make toast, combine. Is there anyone who doesn't love this speedy life saver?

This recipe isn't complicated. It is time consuming as the beans really are baked, unlike the tinned varieties. Don't worry though, a few minutes chopping and combining and you can leave the dish to do its thing in the oven. A little effort turns this everyday fare into something rather more interesting. You can jar the finished dish if you like and have homemade proper baked beans on hand in your store cupboard, although I tend to freeze them in batches instead. The choice is yours. I hope you give them a try.

You will need dried beans for this recipe and a casserole dish with a 3.5 L capacity.

Ingredients

200g dried haricot or cannellini beans
3 tbsp extra-virgin olive oil
1 large or 2 small onions, finely diced
2 garlic cloves, finely crushed
400g can chopped tomatoes
1 tbsp Tomato puree
1 tbsp concentrated apple juice
(or 1 tbsp dark brown sugar)

3 tbsp cider vinegar
A few shakes of Worcestershire sauce
1 bay leaf
1 tsp Dijon mustard
½ tsp mixed spice
½ tsp paprika
Grated cheese of your choice to serve
1 tsp chilli (add to spice mix if you fancy a spicier version)

Method

Soak the beans in water overnight (you can use canned beans but this results in an overcooked end dish). Drain them, place in a pan, cover with fresh water and bring to the boil over a medium heat. Cook for about 45 mins to 1 hour until tender. Or, follow the instructions for your pressure cooker (check, as times vary).

Remove from the heat and set aside to cool. Reserve 100ml of the cooking liquor then drain well.

Heat the oil in a large saucepan over a medium heat, add the onions and cook for 6-8 minutes, until soft and translucent.

Top Tip

If you have a pressure cooker, cook the beans according to instructions. It will speed up the process.

Add a teaspoon or two of chilli for chilli beans, or curry powder for curried beans!

Add the garlic, tomato puree, mustard, Worcestershire sauce, cider vinegar, apple concentrate (or sugar) and spices into the reserved cooking liquor and mix well. Season to taste.

Stir the spice mixture, with the tomatoes and 400ml water, into the onions. At this stage, you can blitz the mix if you wanted a smooth sauce. Add the beans, the bay leaf and heat the mixture through in the pan until the liquid is starting to bubble.

Transfer the beans to a casserole dish and pre-heat the oven to 140°C/120°C fan/gas mark 1. Cover and cook for 2½-3 hours, stirring a few times. Once ready, you should have a thick sauce and tender beans.

Serve the beans on toasted, buttered, Soda or Sourdough bread with grated cheese, if you like.

Proper Baked Beans

Chestnut & Tofu Sausages

This recipe owes its creation to a guesthouse in County Cork, Ireland. Their veggie breakfast sausages were the stuff of legend. Here's my own interpretation, which has become a family favourite, and is often preferred to the meat versions.

Use pre-cooked (or vacuum-packed) chestnuts, firm tofu and a hard, strong cheddar or similar. The sausages are actually easier to cook, or more accurately turn, if they are done from frozen.

Ingredients

400g chestnuts
250g firm tofu, mashed
1 onion, grated
1 small garlic clove, crushed
2½ tsp finely chopped fresh sage
1 tsp finely chopped fresh rosemary
1 tsp thyme leaves
130g strong hard cheese, such as cheddar, gruyere or parmesan which has been grated

1 tsp yeast extract
1 tsp vegetable bouillon
½ tsp freshly ground black pepper
1 egg, beaten
200 - 250g fine brown breadcrumbs

Method

Put the chestnuts in a food processor and pulse to get a fine crumbly texture.

Transfer the processed chestnuts into a bowl and add the rest of the ingredients, except the breadcrumbs.

Now add only enough breadcrumbs to get a firm consistency that can be shaped.

Wet your hands and form the mixture into sausage shapes.

Store in the freezer. The best way to do this is to place a few in plastic freezer bags, or airtight tubs, with baking parchment separating the sausage layers.

To cook, add a little oil to a non-stick frying pan and cook the sausages for 7 -10 minutes, turning frequently until browned.

They will cook in the oven too but may dry out a little.

Glamorgan Sausages

The provenance of these delightful cheesy treats is much debated; although they are certainly Welsh, their birth is shrouded in mystery. However they came to us, and whatever the debate, they are tasty fare. I always double the recipe and freeze half.

Makes 6 sausages.

Ingredients

100g leeks (or 1 large leek), well washed and finely diced

170g fresh breadcrumbs, a mixture of white and brown if available

2 tsp thyme, finely chopped

2 tsp parsley, finely chopped

2 eggs, separated

1½ tsp English mustard

½ tsp paprika

Nutmeg, to taste

150g Caerphillly

30g Cheddar

2 tbsp milk

50g flour

Method

Melt half the butter in a frying pan and sweat the leeks over a medium heat until well softened. Season well with salt, pepper and nutmeg.

Mix 100g breadcrumbs with the thyme and paprika.

Crumble the Caerphilly and grate the cheddar into the breadcrumb mixture and stir in the leeks.

Beat the egg yolks and mustard together, add to the breadcrumb mix and season well.

Wet your hands and shape the mixture into six sausages. Chill the sausages for 30 minutes

Heat the oven to 180C/160C fan/gas 4.

Whisk the egg whites until frothy.

Top Tip

I sometimes use oats for the coating (instead of breadcrumbs) as a kind of Welsh/Scottish union!

Place the flour, egg whites and remaining breadcrumbs on separate plates, or trays. Roll each sausage in the flour, then the egg whites, then breadcrumbs to coat.

Melt the remaining butter or oil in the pan over a medium-high heat. When hot, add the sausages and cook until just golden on each side. Transfer to a baking sheet and cook for about 20 minutes, until richly golden.

Serve immediately.

I like to serve them on their own with a relish on the side, although they match well with a traditional breakfast.

You can deep fry them, if you prefer, for a very crunchy golden treat.

DIY Muesli

Not so much a recipe as a suggestion list, this is a fun breakfast to encourage children to eat something healthier than 'Coco Pops'. Adults usually enjoy building their own breakfast pot pourri too.

I keep everything in tubs and jars and put it on the table for everyone to help themselves. Young children may need a hand so they get a balanced mix.

If you do find you enjoy this, reusing airtight glass jars, and investing in some basic ingredients, will mean you can make it anytime from your cupboard staples.

If you find a mix that works for everyone, you could make up a larger quantity. As a rough guide use 200g of porridge oats to 50g of the other ingredients (25g bran). This will make around 8 portions.

Decant to an airtight storage container so you can serve it without having to mix the separate components.

To ring the changes you can soak the nuts overnight for a different texture. Basically anything goes, so experiment!

Ingredients

Base
Porridge Oats
Toasted Rye Flakes
Flaked Bran or wheatgerm
Seeds and Nuts
Sunflower seeds
Pumpkin seeds
Linseed
Sesame seed
Almonds
hazelnuts

Fruit
Apricots
Figs
Cranberries
Coconut nibs
Freshly grated apple

To serve
Plain yoghurt
Honey

Method

Take a few spoonfuls of the porridge oats, then add the other base ingredients. Add the fruit, seeds and nuts according to taste. To finish dollop with yoghurt and honey.

Served topped with fresh fruit, when available.

Breakfast Muffins

Sorry if you were thinking chocolate. These are a savoury muffin rather than a sweet one, based on classic flavours that work well together. Once you've mastered the basic recipe you can always play around with the combos using different cheeses or types of onion, adding bacon as well, or instead of the sun-dried tomatoes. Make sure you keep to the recipe ratios to avoid any disasters.

You will need a 12 hole (or 2 x 6 hole) deep muffin tin.

Ingredients

50g sun-dried tomatoes
(from a jar, drained and chopped)
1 red onion, finely diced
250g wholemeal self-raising flour
2 tsp baking powder
½ tsp bicarbonate of soda
¼ tsp salt
1 tbsp milk

2 eggs
80g unsalted butter, melted and cooled
(you can use oil instead)
200ml yoghurt
100g strong cheddar, grated
75g Parmesan or similar
1 tbsp finely chopped chives (optional)

Method

Heat the oven to 200C/180C Fan/400F/gas mark 6 and line a muffin tin with 12 paper cases.

Warm the oil over a medium heat and fry the onion until just softened, about five minutes, then set aside to cool.

In a large bowl, whisk together the flour, baking powder, bicarbonate of soda and salt. In a jug, whisk the eggs, butter and yoghurt.

Stir that into the flour mixture with a spatula until just combined. Then fold in the cooled onions, sundried tomatoes and chives (if using) and two-thirds of the cheese until just evenly distributed. Add milk if it seems dry - it should form a stiff mix that doesn't easily drop off a spoon.

Spoon the mixture into the muffin tin, sprinkle on the rest of the cheese, and bake for about 18 minutes, until the tops are golden and a cake tester or skewer comes out clean.

Top Tip

Don't over-mix this batter. Lightly combine the wet and dry ingredients and don't worry about lumps!

Peppers & Eggs (or Shakshuka)

I've been making this recipe for decades; long before Shakshuka became ubiquitous in chain restaurants. Piperade, a Basque dish, is very similar. Whatever you call it, it's tasty fare for breakfast or brunch.

Ingredients

2 large onions, thinly sliced
2 red peppers, cut into long slices
2 green peppers, cut into long slices
4 garlic cloves, finely chopped
½ tsp cumin seeds
½ tsp cayenne pepper
1 tbsp tomato purée

2 x 400g tins tomatoes
1 small bunch fresh coriander, roughly chopped
1 small bunch fresh parsley, roughly chopped
8 free-range eggs
85g/3oz feta, crumbled
8 tbsp thick natural yoghurt or labneh*
salt and freshly ground black pepper
* *Middle-Eastern soft cheese*

Method

Heat a generous amount of olive oil in a large, lidded frying pan (if you don't have a lid, cover the pan with baking parchment or foil). Add the onions and peppers and season with salt and pepper. Cook covered on a medium heat until softened (15-20 minutes). Add the garlic and cook for a further 2 minutes.

Sprinkle in the cumin and cayenne pepper. Stir in the tomato purée and cook for a couple more minutes until the paste starts to separate. Add the tomatoes with a splash of water.

Uncover and simmer for 10 minutes, until reduced a little. Taste after 5 minutes and add a little sugar if you think the tomatoes are too acidic. Keep an eye on the texture – you don't want it watery, but it mustn't dry out too much either. Add another splash of water if necessary. When the sauce is reduced, stir in the herbs (reserve a few for decoration).

Make 8 small wells in the sauce. Break an egg into a ramekin or cup and drop carefully into a well, repeat with the all the eggs. Cover and cook for a few more minutes until the whites are just set and the yolks are still runny. Sprinkle over the crumbled feta. You could add cooked chorizo if you prefer.

Serve with flatbreads or bread of your choice for mopping up any remaining sauce.

Huevos Rancheros

A Mexican inspired breakfast dish, literally ranch eggs. There are many versions and you can simplify it or pimp it up as much as you like. I like to serve it with the traditional 'refried beans' as it makes it a more substantial meal. The avocado is not essential but makes a nice contrast. I sometimes cook the salsa to ring the changes, and often leave out the cheese.

Serves 4

Ingredients

1 small onion, diced
2 garlic cloves, crushed
400g black beans, drained and rinsed
1 tsp ground cumin
¼ tsp chilli powder
½ tsp dried oregano
4 eggs

4 small flour tortillas, warmed
1 large tomato, diced
1 small green chilli
30g cheddar, grated
To serve:
1 avocado, peeled, de-stoned and diced
1 lime, half juiced, half cut into wedges, chopped coriander

Method

Heat 1 tablespoon of oil in a large pan. Add the onions with a pinch of salt, and cook until translucent, around 5 mins. Add the garlic and cook for a minute more.

Stir in the beans, cumin, chilli powder, oregano, some seasoning and 100ml water. Cook for 5-7 mins, stirring occasionally, or until the beans have softened, then remove from the heat, mash and set aside.

Chop the tomato, and chili and place in a bowl. Add a squeeze of lime and some fresh coriander. Set aside.

Heat the remaining oil in a large frying pan over a medium-high heat. Crack in the eggs, then reduce the heat to low and cook slowly until the whites are completely firm.

Meanwhile warm through the tortilla in the oven or microwave.

To assemble the dish, spread the refried beans onto the tortillas, add the tomato salsa and eggs and sprinkle with cheese.

To garnish, top with some avocado, a squeeze of lime juice and the rest of the fresh coriander.

If you fancy having a go at making your own tortilla it's quite straightforward. My method is on page 40.

Breakfasts & Brunches

Huevos Rancheros

Fried Tomato Bread

This is a recipe for summer, when you have a glut of ripe tomatoes. I like to use a mixture of cherry tomatoes as it looks so cheerful in the pan. It's barely a recipe, but I don't offer any apologies for this simple summer fare. You will need a large non-stick frying pan.

Ingredients

300g mixed cherry tomatoes, cut in half
1 slice of wholemeal or sourdough bread – a day old is best
Basil
1 tspn Balsamic vinegar
½ garlic clove crushed (optional)
Seasoning

Method

This is a simple, slow cooked dish. The trick is to use a lot of olive oil and let the tomatoes cook down slowly until they are soft and threatening to collapse. Add the garlic (if using) once the tomatoes have cooked a bit, with a little more oil if necessary. Add the balsamic and seasoning.

Once the tomatoes start to release their juices, push them to one side and place the bread in the pan; press it into the juices. Allow it to soak up the tomato juice and oil. Once it is starting to crisp and brown, turn it over and repeat the process. Serve the tomatoes on the bread and garnish with the basil.

Tattie Scones

This is an essential item on a traditional Scottish breakfast, but a lot of places in the UK have their own version of this potato scone or cake. It's simple to make and a whole lot better than the commercial versions, which include wholly unnecessary ingredients. I often deliberately make extra mash so I can make them. They freeze well, so make a big batch.

Ingredients

450g floury potatoes, peeled and cooked - the "tattie" in the title.
½ tsp salt
2oz butter
4oz self raising flour

Method

Mash potatoes, add salt and butter and enough flour to give a stiff mixture. You may not need it all.

Turn out onto floured surface, knead lightly and roll into a round about 1cm thick. You can use a saucer as a template, although a rustic look is fine.

Cut into triangles and cook on a medium hot, lightly greased griddle (or non-stick pan) for 3-5 min on each side.

Serve hot with other breakfast items of your choice.

Buckwheat Pancakes

I first discovered buckwheat pancakes courtesy of Sarah Brown's Vegetarian Kitchen in 1980's and have been making them ever since. The original recipe makes great pancakes, but is not gluten free, so I developed these gluten free alternatives. Although slightly heavier than the originals, they are still delicious and can be used as a substitute for any pancake recipe containing wheat. I later discovered, when staying in Brittany in 1986, that the Brettons make a buckwheat pancake called Galettes De Sarrasin. They are essentially the same thing.

Ingredients

100g buckwheat flour
pinch of salt
1 egg
300ml milk
50g butter, melted

Method

Place the flour, salt, egg and half the milk into a bowl or jug.

Beat to a smooth paste then stir in the remaining milk, enough to make a thin batter.

Refrigerate the batter for up to 12 hours, which gives a better flavour, or if using straight away leave at room temperature for at least an hour.

Lightly oil a frying pan so that the oil just covers the surface and get the pan nice and hot.

Stir the melted butter into the batter then pour or spoon some batter into the hot pan and roll it out to the edges.

Cook the pancake, loosening the edges, until the base is golden.

Turn it over and cook the other side. Repeat until the batter is used.

Serve with a topping or filling of your choice. In Brittany, they often use this galette as a vehicle for a savoury filling. Great for a weekend brunch.

Buckwheat Pancakes

Scotch Pancakes

I often knock these up for a leisurely Sunday morning breakfast. Plain or spiced, with butter or fruit or yoghurt, or any combination you can think of. Easier to make than a traditional pancake, they hold well in a tea towel in a warm oven. Easily double or triple the recipe to feed a hungry crowd.

It will help if you have a cast iron girdle. In Scotland, they're called girdles, not griddles. These were hung above an open fire 170 years ago and are still used today, although more commonly on a stove top. Any heavy-based pan that holds the heat will do.

Ingredients

200g plain flour
1 tbsp baking powder
Pinch of salt
1 large egg
300ml milk
You can add a spoon of sugar if you want a sweet version

Method

Add the dry ingredients to a mixing bowl.

Beat the egg and milk into dry mixture to form a thick batter.

Heat the frying pan to a medium heat and add oil.

Fry a ladleful of batter till bubbling and golden. Flip and cook on the second side.

Make sure you don't have the pan too hot or the outside will cook before the middle is done.

Place in a tea towel in a warm oven to keep them hot and continue to cook the pancakes until all the batter is used.

Serve with your chosen topping.

Porridge Pancakes

If you're one of those people who make too much porridge, or like me, finds your partner leaves the house without eating their share, then this recipe is for you. They are very similar to the previous Scotch pancakes, with the added bonus of knowing you're virtuously using up leftovers. I appreciate they might not sound especially delicious, but believe me they are. If you never have any leftover porridge, consider making some extra so you can try this recipe. I promise you won't be disappointed. They're surprisingly light, very tasty, and will fill you up.

Like the Scotch pancakes, keep them warm in a low oven wrapped in a clean tea towel whilst you complete the batch. They work well cooked on a girdle, but a heavy-duty non-stick frying pan will do.

Serve with butter, maple syrup, fruit and yoghurt or your choice of adornment. They make a great substitute for blinis, if you're feeling adventurous.

Ingredients

150g cooked, cooled, porridge - If you have a little more or less, adjust the quantity of flour so the total is 300g. You must have at least 100g of flour in the mix
150g self raising flour; I use brown, but white works fine
2 large eggs
100ml - 300ml milk; enough to make a smooth batter thick enough to coat a spoon without sliding off immediately. If it's too thin they will spread and be too thin.
2 tsp baking powder

Method

Put the porridge in a bowl and combine with the other ingredients, except the milk. Add a little milk at a time until you have a smooth batter that doesn't spread too quickly in the pan. I blitz mine with a high speed hand blender but elbow grease will work just as well.

Heat a heavy pan or girdle, wiped with a little vegetable oil. Once hot, add the batter in spoonfuls. Your pan size will determine how many you can cook in one batch.

Cook over a medium heat until bubbles appear in the batter and the underside is evenly browned. Flip and cook the other side.

Make sure the pan maintains a medium heat or the underside will cook and brown before the middle of the pancake is cooked.

Transfer to a clean tea towel and keep warm in a low oven until you've used up all the batter.

Breakfast Smoothie

This is a good breakfast if you're in a rush and not accustomed to eating, first thing. It can even be made the night before, but add a squeeze of lemon juice if you do, otherwise the bananas will oxidise to an unappetising brown/grey sludge!

This is a much better bet than a supermarket smoothie, as it contains whole fruit rather than juice and the oats help to slow down the sugar release. The milk, nuts and seeds introduce protein which will help fill you up more than a fruit juice concoction.

Once you have the basic idea, you can add whatever you fancy. Coconut milk, nut or grain milks, different nuts, seeds and fruit will all ring the changes.

You will need a high speed blender, hand blender or liquidiser to make this.

Ingredients

75g porridge oats
5 almonds
1 tbsp mixed seeds (you can buy these ready-made or mix your own)
2 large or 3 small bananas, broken into chunks
1 ripe mango, peeled and diced
Handful of soft fruit (I use a frozen mix)
250ml milk (ANY milk)
Honey/yoghurt optional

Method

Blitz the dry ingredients first; the oats, nuts and seeds until they are powdery with no large bits.

Add the fruit and milk (honey and yoghurt if using) and blitz again until smooth.

Serve in tall glasses and enjoy. Add ice if you like, but if you use frozen fruit, this will make a lovely chilled drink.

As long as you follow these rough proportions you can put pretty much anything into your smoothie, but make sure that there's enough carbs and protein to keep you feeling fuller for longer.

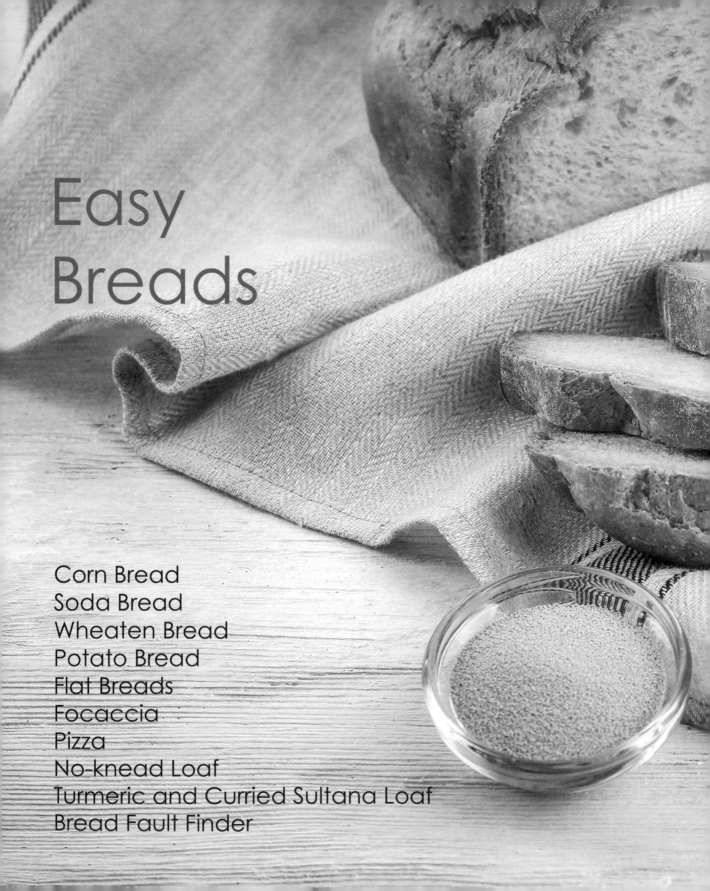

Easy Breads

There is a lot of mystique surrounding bread making. As someone who makes their living making bread, I think this is misplaced. I won't pretend that making bread is all plain sailing and without its challenges. Dough is a living thing and as such has its quirks and preferences. However, I firmly believe that everyone can make edible, tasty bread, simply and without hassle. I've not bothered getting over technical here, but the next section explains some common terms we bread bakers use.

If you get hooked on bread, as I hope you will, you'll discover the more complex and interesting aspects of this 'science' yourself and there are plenty of technical tomes out there you can refer to.

As long as you remember a few basics and follow recipes exactly to begin with, you'll soon be turning out bread like a Home Cook! Practice will increase your confidence and if things do go wrong, it's not the end of the world. In its simplest and noblest form, bread consists of flour, salt, yeast and water, and is one of the cheapest and best things you can make at home.

For ease, all the recipes use 'easy blend' or 'instant' dried yeast which is mixed directly into the dried ingredients. There is no need to mix it with water first. I use cold water from the tap, not warm water, as most modern kitchens are an adequate temperature to get things underway and it dispenses with the need to use a thermometer to check temperatures. Extreme cold retards yeast; extreme heat will kill it.

I weigh the water on a scale for accuracy, as jug measures can vary by 10% or more.

Always add the water a bit at a time rather than all at once. Flour type, age and room temperature can all affect how much water is needed.

If you're not used to kneading, spend an extra 5 minutes making sure the gluten is working and the dough is nice and stretchy. Do it with your hands so you get used to the feel of the dough. Once you're more proficient you can use a stand mixer with a dough hook if you like, but never use a high speed mixer as it makes the dough too hot and can kill the yeast.

A lot of bread books will tell you to use clingfilm to cover the dough whilst it proves, but as I don't use clingfilm, for environmental reasons, I tend to use an oiled container with a lid, or a clean, slightly damp tea towel.

I've included a few pointers at the end of the chapter in case the worst happens and you have a sunken or holey loaf and want to try and find out what went wrong. Very few loaves are inedible, whatever happens!

So roll up your sleeves and get kneading!

A Brief Natter about Terms and Techniques

If you've not made bread before it can seem daunting as there seems to be a whole language around bread making. Here are some of the common terms you will come across and what they mean.

Kneading - Works the dough by pulling, stretching and turning to develop the gluten making a springy pliable dough. You will develop your own style. If you're new to bread, put the mixed ingredients onto a clean, floured counter top and push the mass away from you with the heel of one had whilst pulling with the other. Turn the dough and pile the top and bottom edges into the middle. Repeat the process; pulling, pushing, turning and piling until you have a springy, bouncy dough that is no longer sticky. If you are working with a 'wet dough' you will usually need to mix it and won't be able to knead it much, unless you use a machine.

Gluten - When flour is mixed with water this makes the gluten in wheat apparent. It is a protein that helps baked goods hold their shape.

Shaping - Although this seems obvious that you're forming the dough into the final bread shape, doing it requires some practice. A long loaf is usually folded into the middle and tucked into a loaf pan and a round loaf is usually turned with one had whilst shaping the sides into a domed form with the other. Don't worry about it though, whatever shape your final loaf, it will taste a lot better than your average supermarket loaf.

Knocking back - Kneading the dough with your hands to push out the air.

Proving - This is the final stage before bread is baked. The dough is left to rise for a second - and usually - final time. It's important to cover the dough at this stage so it doesn't form a crust. You can tell when the dough is ready by gently pressing it and seeing if it springs back. Don't let the dough over-prove.

Corn Bread

A naturally gluten free bread, this is has a cakey texture and is great for dunking into sauce and soups. It's quick to make and hard to get wrong, so give it a go. I often make a huge batch of veggie chilli and add some just-out-of-the-oven corn bread for a substantial supper to feed a crowd.

Ingredients

250g fine cornmeal or maize meal
2 tsp gluten-free baking powder
½ tsp bicarbonate of soda
1 tsp fine salt
½ tsp chilli powder
75g strong cheddar, grated
100ml plain whole-milk yoghurt
200ml whole milk

Method

Heat the oven to 200C/180C Fan/Gas 6 and butter a 1.5-litre oven dish or tin.

Mix the cornmeal, baking powder, bicarbonate of soda and salt in a large bowl, then stir in the cheese and chilli.

Whisk together the milk and yoghurt, and stir into the mix until well combined. Don't overbeat the mixture though.

Pour into the tin and bake for 25 minutes, until firm and golden on top. Leave to cool a little, and serve while still warm.

Freezes well for a couple of months if well wrapped.

Once you've mastered the basic recipe you can add ingredients to spice things up. Bacon, sun-dried tomatoes, onions and cheese all work well.

Soda Bread

Another quick, un-yeasted bread. Soda bread was part of my childhood; served in thick slabs, fresh out of the oven, and plastered in butter. I hope you'll be delighted to add it to your repertoire.

Ingredients
500g plain flour
2 tsp bicarbonate of soda
1 tsp fine sea salt
400ml live yoghurt
A little milk, if necessary, to loosen

Method
Heat the oven to 200°C/180C Fan/Gas 6.

Sift the flour and bicarbonate of soda into a large mixing bowl and stir in the salt.

Make a well in the centre and pour in the yoghurt. If necessary, add a tablespoon or two of milk to bring the mixture together; it should form a soft, slightly sticky dough.

Tip it out on to a lightly-floured work surface and knead lightly for about a minute, just long enough to pull it together into a loose ball, but no longer. Forget what you think you know about bread. Don't work this like bread dough or you'll end up with rock hard, barely risen loaf. It needs to go into the oven whilst the bicarbonate of soda is still reacting with the live yoghurt.

Put the round of dough on a lightly-floured baking sheet and dust with flour. Mark a deep cross in it with a sharp, serrated knife, cutting at least half way through the loaf.

Put it in a preheated and bake for 40-45 minutes, until the loaf sounds hollow when tapped underneath.

Cool on a wire rack if you like a crunchy crust, or wrap in a clean tea tea towel if you prefer a softer crust.

This bread is best eaten while still warm, spread with butter.

Easy Breads

Soda Bread

Wheaten Bread

This is effectively soda bread made with wholewheat flour. It's a traditional Northern Irish recipe and I'm using a recipe I've adapted from one given to me by a Northern Irish friend. You can bake it on a baking tray instead of a loaf tin, but cook it for 5 minutes less.

Unlike soda bread, traditional wheaten bread is often slightly sweet. The flour itself adds a malty sweetness to the bread and this is accentuated by the addition of sugar. If you prefer a more savoury version, simply leave it out.

*Although buttermilk is traditionally used, live yoghurt works just as well if you can't get hold of it. I've weighed the liquid as it makes the recipe more accurate.

Ingredients
285g coarse wholemeal flour
90g Plain flour
30g caster sugar
1 tsp baking powder
¾ tsp baking soda
¼ tsp salt
40g buttter
2 eggs
285g buttermilk*

Method
Preheat oven to 200°C/180C Fan/Gas 6. Grease a 2LB loaf tin and line with parchment paper.

In a large bowl, mix together the flours, sugar, baking powder, baking soda and salt. Rub in the butter until the mix resembles breadcrumbs.

In a separate bowl, whisk together the eggs and buttermilk. Make a well in the flour mixture, and pour in the liquid.

Mix together just until all the flour is moistened. Be careful not to over-mix.

Scoop the batter into the tin and lightly flatten the top.

Bake in the preheated oven for 30-35 minutes, until a skewer comes out clean and the top is golden. You want to make sure the bread is fully baked, without becoming dry.

Allow the loaf to cool in the tin for a few minutes before removing to a rack.

Cover with a tea towel so the loaf doesn't dry out.

Serve immediately.

Best used on the day of baking but will toast or freeze well.

Easy Breads

Bread made with potatoes is evident in most European cuisines. From Irish farls, to German kartoffelbrot and many others. This recipe is of Eastern European origin. It's made with mashed potatoes so you need a floury, fluffy potato for good results. This bread has a moist and springy crumb and is fairly dense. It won't rise like most yeasted breads as the potatoes are dense and retard the proving process, but it's an easy tasty bread, which is surprisingly light.

As this is the first loaf we've tried which is yeasted, I've gone into some detail about how to knead and shape the loaf.

Ingredients

500g floury potatoes (e.g. Maris Piper) peeled and cut into chunks
2 tsp dried yeast
300g strong white flour
75g strong wholewheat flour
1 ½ tsp salt
175ml liquid reserved from cooking the potatoes

Method

Boil the potatoes in plenty of water until cooked, reserving 175ml of the cooking liquid to a jug when you drain them.

Mash thoroughly with a fork or masher. If you have a ricer, this will give best results. Lumps are your enemy here.

Leave aside until they are cool and the water is tepid. If they get cold, that's fine.

Put the flour in a bowl and add the yeast. Make a well in the centre and add the enough of the reserved cooking liquid - about 100 mls or so - to make a paste with a little of the flour.

Use a wooden spoon to draw enough flour into the water to make the paste. Cover the bowl with a tea towel and allow this mixture to bubble and froth for 20 minutes. This is a 'sponge' starter and will improve both the taste and texture of your finished loaf.

Now add the cooled mash and salt to the mixture and enough of the remaining potato water to form a soft and moist dough.

Turn the dough onto a lightly floured surface and need for 10 -15 minutes until smooth, soft and shiny. Put the dough in a clean bowl, covered with a tea towel, or in a oiled tub with a lid, and leave to rise for around 2 hours, The dough should have doubled in size. Leave it a little longer if it isn't.

Punch the air out of the risen dough (knocking back) and leave to rest for 10 minutes.

The dough will now be ready to shape into a loaf. You could use a greased 2LB loaf tin, but the authentic shape for this bread is a round free-form loaf.

Easy Breads

Press your fingers into the base of the dough, whilst holding it with both hands. Rotate the dough, exerting a light pressure with your fingertips, whilst at the same time tucking the sides of the dough underneath the to form the base of the loaf. Form the dough into a rough ball and cup your hand around it, applying gentle pressure, whilst simultaneously rotating it. You'll get the hang of it the more you do it.

Place the dough face down on the work surface and continue the turning and tucking in a steady clockwise motion. The dough should be smooth and round. Turn it over so the base is now the top and pinch the seam together. Place the loaf, seam side down, on a lightly floured baking tray covered with a clean dry tea towel.

Leave to rise again (or "prove") until the dough is well-risen and springs back when you press it gently with a finger. This will take around half an hour but could be longer if temperatures in your kitchen are cool.

Dust the risen loaf lightly with flour and cut three parallel slashes 1cm deep one way and then the other to make a criss-cross pattern. You can get a special tool to do this but a sharp, serrated knife works well.

Bake in a preheated oven - 220C/200C Fan/Gas 7 - for 45 minutes to one hour until crispy and hollow sounding when the base is tapped.

If you've cooked this bread in a loaf tin it may need tipping out, inverting and returning (inverted) to the loaf tin and then put back into the oven for a further 5 minutes until it is cooked, but check it first.

Leave on a wire rack until cool. Covering it with a tea towel will trap the steam and give you a softer crust. For a crusty loaf, leave uncovered until cool.

Flat Breads

Flat bread describes a range of breads, with and without yeast, that as their name suggests, do not rise substantlally In helght. Every culture has Its own, from MIddle Eastern Maneesh to the ubiquitous Italian Pizza and Focaccia, which are technically 'flatbreads'. Pitta, naan and tortilla also come under this broad heading.

Here, I will give you an all purpose recipe that can be used in a variety of ways, stuffed, topped, in a salad, toasted, dipped in something like hummus, or used to mop up juices. In fact, its uses are endless, so get baking.

Flat breads can be cooked in a cast-iron pan, or heavy-based frying pan, or if you have neither, some like naan and pitta can be cooked under a very hot grill - though be careful they don't catch too much.

This will make up to 12 flat breads depending on the size you roll them out to. The dough, once its proved, can be frozen, or you can make the flatbreads and cook them and then freeze them, separated by baking parchment. They are prone to getting busted up in the freezer, so protect them well.

Basic Flat Bread Dough

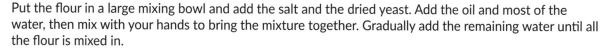

Ingredients

300g strong white bread flour
200g plain flour
10g salt
10g instant yeast
2 tbsp olive oil
300ml water

Method

Put the flour in a large mixing bowl and add the salt and the dried yeast. Add the oil and most of the water, then mix with your hands to bring the mixture together. Gradually add the remaining water until all the flour is mixed in.

Put the dough on a lightly-floured board and knead for around 10 minutes. Err on the side of doing this for the full time if you are new to kneading.

When the dough feels smooth and silky, place it back in the mixing bowl, cover it with a tea towel and leave it in a warm place to rise for at least an hour. The dough should have roughly doubled in size.

Tip the dough out on to a lightly-floured surface, fold repeatedly until all the air is knocked out of it, then tear it into 12 equal pieces. At this stage allow the dough to rest, covered, for up to 10 minutes to relax the dough. It will make it easier to roll.

Roll each piece into a ball. Flatten each ball with a rolling pin to 16-18cm.

Cook in a preheated pan, without oil, on a medium heat, turning as they start to brown. Maximum of a couple of minutes each side. Place into a tea towel in a low oven whilst you cook the rest of the batch.

To oven cook Preheat the oven to 220°C/200°C Fan/Gas 7. Place the bread on a baking tray, prick a few times with a fork and cook for around 8 minutes until puffed and brown in places.

To grill, turn the grill to high and pre-heat. Brush the bread with a little oil and place on a heavy-duty baking tray. Grill until they start to rise and colour. Turn over and repeat. The flat breads only take a few minutes to cook.

Focaccia

Another Italian classic, this dough is wetter than the pizza dough and consequently a little more difficult to handle. However, it is still an easy and satisfying bread to make. Don't be tempted to add lots of extra flour or you'll end up with a different sort of bread.

Ingredients

7g dried yeast
500g strong white flour
75ml olive oil and extra for drizzling
1½ tsp fine sea salt
250ml water
50g olives
Rosemary, sage or oregano leaves

Method

Mix the flour, yeast and salt in a large bowl, and make a well in the centre. Pour in 75ml of the extra-virgin olive oil and 250ml water.

Mix to form a soft dough, adding a splash more warm water if required.

Now knead the dough, on a clean lightly-floured surface, for 10 to 15 minutes until smooth and elastic.

Shape into a round and place in a lightly oiled bowl. Cover the dough with a damp tea-towel and leave in a warm place for an hour or until the dough has doubled in size.

Knock back the dough and shape it into a round or oblong. You will need to press it out with your hands as it will be too wet to roll out. I usually press it into a well-floured oblong tin (about 35cm x 23cm) but you can place it on a baking sheet if you prefer.

Preheat the oven to 220C/Fan 200C/Gas 7.

Press your fingers all over the dough to make dimples and scatter with the mixed olives and herbs of your choice. Drizzle with another 1 tablespoon of oil and scatter with sea salt.

Cover loosely with a clean, dry tea-towel and leave to rise for another 30 minutes until doubled in size and the dimples are pronounced and puffy.

Cook until golden, about 20 minutes.

Pizza

This classic Italian flat bread has as many recipes as there are days in the year. Some of the commercial offerings are a sad travesty of this original freshly made, thin-crusted delight. At home, we make a slightly more bready pizza to cope with the copious toppings. You can experiment to make something that suits your own style, and how you like to eat pizza. This basic recipe will make 2 large pizza to serve 6- 8, or four smaller ones. We often use two large rectangular baking tins rather than shaping round pizzas. The choice is yours. Whatever you decide, once you've seen how easy it is to make, and how tasty to eat, you won't buy a takeaway!

Ingredients

Dough:
1kg white bread flour or Tipo Italian '00' flour if you can get it
2 x 7g dried yeast sachets
2 tbsp extra virgin olive oil
1 tsp fine sea salt

Tomato Sauce:
1 x 400g tin of quality plum tomatoes
1 clove of garlic
fresh basil
olive oil

Topping:
Fresh basil leaves
100g Mozzarella

Easy Breads

Method

Sieve the flour and salt into large bowl and make a well in the middle.

In a jug, mix the yeast and oil into 650ml of tap water and pour into the well.

Gradually bring the flour in from the sides to mix it into the liquid. Keep mixing, drawing larger amounts of flour in, and when it all starts to come together, turn out on to a clean work surface and work the rest of the flour in with your clean, flour-dusted hands.

Knead until you have a smooth, springy dough (10-15 minutes). You can do this in a mixer with a dough hook, but always finish off by hand so you get to feel the dough is the right texture.

Place the dough in a large lightly-oiled bowl and turn over so the top has a light coating of oil.

Cover the bowl with a damp cloth and place in a warm room for about an hour until the dough has doubled in size.

In the meantime make the tomato sauce.

Peel and finely slice the garlic.

Heat 1 tablespoon of oil in a pan on a medium-low heat, add the garlic and cook gently for a couple of minutes, or until the garlic is lightly golden, then add the tomatoes, and a pinch of salt and pepper.
Leave the sauce to simmer gently for around 20 minutes, or until smooth, breaking up the tomatoes with a wooden spoon. You can blitz it if you prefer a smoother sauce, or use ready made passata. Allow to cool.

Dust a clean worktop with flour and knead the dough a bit to push the air out with your hands.

You can either use it immediately, or keep it, wrapped in an oiled container or plastic bag, in the fridge until required. If using straight away, divide the dough up into as many little balls as you want to make pizzas – this amount of dough is enough to make about six to eight medium pizzas or you can halve and freeze the remainder. See tip for freezing pizza dough.

Roll the pizzas out about 15 minutes before you want to cook them. Don't leave them for too long or they'll form a dried out covering.

Top with the tomato sauce, torn basil leaves and mozarella.

When you're ready to cook them, preheat the oven to 250°C/220°C fan/gas 9 or the hottest it will go. This is the key to a crispy base.

At this stage you can apply your topping: spread the tomato sauce over the base, spreading it out to the edges. Tear over the mozzarella and scatter with the remaining basil leaves. Drizzle with a tiny bit of olive oil and add a pinch of salt and pepper. Add toppings as desired,but don't overdo it or you crispy pizza will be no more!

If you have a pizza tile or plain unglazed terracotta tile, you will get a crispier result, but if not a thin baking sheet is fine. You may not get such a crispy result but they will taste fine. Cook for 7 to 10 minutes, until the pizzas are golden and crispy.

I often leave the dough overnight to develop the flavour. I also often halve this batch and store one half in the freezer to defrost and use another time. Store in an airtight container.

Easy Breads

No-Knead Loaf

This bread takes time, but not a lot of effort. It's a great beginner's loaf and gives reliable, tasty results. Once you've done it a couple of times, you'll be able to adjust the timings to get a perfect loaf for breakfast, lunch or tea. Even if you're a more experienced bread maker, you might enjoy trying this for fun.

Ingredients

300g strong white bread flour
100g strong wholemeal bread flour, plus extra for dusting
7g salt
1 tsp easy-bake yeast
300ml lukewarm water
fat for greasing

Method

Place the flours, salt and yeast in a good size bowl, keeping the salt away from the yeast. Combine with your hand or a wooden spoon.

Make a well in the flour. Pour in all of the water.

Mix the flour into the liquid to make the dough. It will be fairly soft and sticky at this stage. Ensure all of the flour has been incorporated.

Prove the dough: cover the bowl with a damp tea towel. Place the covered bowl somewhere cool (around 15/16 degrees, but not in a draft), to allow the dough to prove slowly.

Prove for about 24 hours or until doubled in size. The time varies according to the temperature.

Top Tip

For a variation, top with seeds of your choice before baking.

Shape the loaf. This may not be possible in the traditional sense as the dough can be very wet and batter-like. You can flour everything really well, including your hands, and ease it into a well-greased and floured 20cm cake tin or a 2LB loaf tin.

Prove again. Cover with a tea towel or plastic bag (making sure they don't touch the dough). Leave for a further 2 hours or until the dough is rising from the tin.

Preheat the oven to 220C/200C Fan/Gas 7.

Place the bread in the centre of the oven, covered with a double layer of foil or a stock pot (or a Dutch oven if you have one) and bake for 20 minutes. Remove the tin foil from the tin. Rotate the tin 180° and return to the oven. Bake for a further 15-20 minutes.

Carefully tip the bread out of the cake tin and tap the base of the bread. It should sound hollow. If not, place the bread, upside down, directly onto the oven shelf and bake for a further 5 minutes, or until it sounds hollow.

Cool on a rack before eating.

Easy Breads

Turmeric and Curried Sultana Bread

I love the colour of this bread and it smells amazing too. It's a very wet dough, but requires little in the way of kneading. I always do an overnight dough for a light and tasty loaf. It's fantastic served with cheese and chutney or as part of a Ploughman's but I've also discovered it is amazing toasted and slathered with butter.

Ingredients

500g strong white flour
1 tsp salt
350ml lukewarm water
½ tsp. Instant yeast
2 level-tsp turmeric powder
1 tbsp olive oil
100g sultanas soaked overnight with
2 tsp curry powder and a little hot water
2 tsp black onion seed or Nigella to decorate the top

Method

Measure all the dry ingredients (except the curry powder, sultanas and seeds) into a bowl. Make a well in the centre of the dried ingredients and add as much of the oil and water as needed to make a really soft dough. At this stage it will be almost sloppy, so if it seems dry once mixed in, add some more.

Cover and leave in the kitchen overnight. The minimum time required is 8 hours. It should be well risen and bubbly.

In the meantime soak the sultanas in a little boiling water and the curry powder. Leave overnight. In the morning, get rid of the excess water and let the sultanas dry on a piece of kitchen towel to soak up any excess moisture.

Next, generously flour your worktop and hands. Turn the dough out using a spatula or your fingers. A couple of dough scrapers make this easier, but are by no means essential.

Flatten the dough in front with your palms, stretching it out to a rough rectangle. See photo 1.

"Dot" with the sultanas.

Now fold the sides of the dough into the centre, over each other, to form a parcel. See photo 2.

Turn the whole thing over, rotating 90°, so the seam is now horizontal. See photo 3.

Flatten it out and fold again from both sides, overlapping in the middle so that the sultanas are well distributed. The dough should now be more manageable. If it's still too wet, work in a little more flour, but try not to add too much.

Shape the dough into a round and place on a baking sheet, or shape into a loaf in a 2LB loaf tin. I sometimes make 2 small loaves and freeze one. See photo 4.

Easy Breads

Let it rise until it doubles in size and feels springy to gentle touch.

Turn the oven on to 210C/190 fan/6.5 gas. Gently brush the top of the loaf with a little milk or water and sprinkle on the seeds.

Bake in the centre of the oven for 20-30 minutes. Check by tapping on the base. If you've used a loaf tin it may take longer. Remove from the tin and turn upside down to cook a little longer. It should be brown all over. If necessary, bake it for another 5-10 minutes. I find that in my fan oven, 22 minutes is usually just right for a shaped loaf on a baking sheet.

Allow to cool on a wire rack.

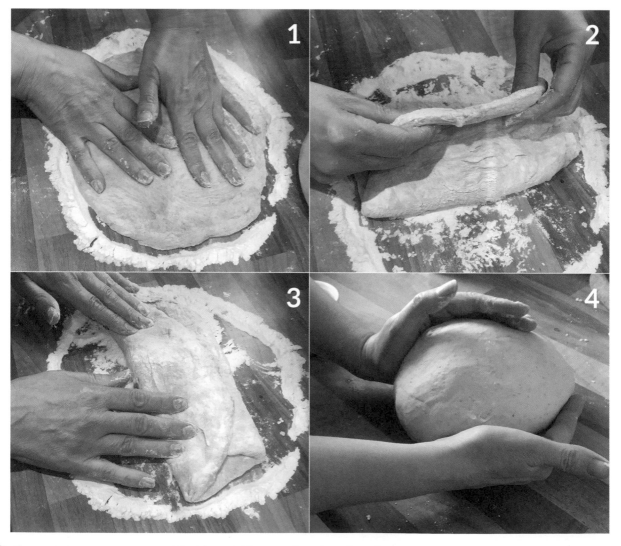

Turmeric & Curried Sultana Bread

Bread Fault Finder

Help! What Went Wrong?

Bread is a living thing. It can be fussy about how it is treated. If we don't treat it well, things can go wrong. It doesn't usually matter, as the end results are invariably edible. However, if you have a loaf that went wrong and want to improve your chances of success next time, this fault finding list might help.

Help! My Loaf Didn't Rise Much

Not enough yeast. Make sure you added the proper amount of yeast to the recipe. As a rare occurrence the yeast can be old or weak. You can check your yeast by adding a teaspoon to some water and leaving it for 15 minutes to see if you get bubbles. If you do, it's fine.

Too much salt in the recipe. Salt controls the activity of the yeast, but too much can really slow it down or, in a worst case scenario, kill it altogether. Use the precise amount in the recipe. Measure accurately. Keep it separate from the yeast.

Under-proving or too short a final rise. This can cause a loaf to fail because the yeast hasn't produced enough gas to fill the tiny pockets that develop in the dough.

Over-proving or too long a final rise time. If you leave the dough for too long, the yeast will run out of energy and the gluten won't be able to hold up the loaf. The result is a loaf that puffs up a bit, or at worst, collapses. Make sure you don't let the dough rise for too long, and not to more than twice the volume it had when you began.

The loaves were put in tins that were too large for them. Make sure you follow the instructions and use the right size tin.

Oven temperature too high. The yeast undergoes a burst of activity during the first few minutes of baking, increasing its production of gases, which are then trapped by the gluten network, producing what is called 'oven spring'. If the oven temperature is too high, the yeast is killed prematurely and 'oven spring' doesn't happen.

Help! My Loaf Spread Out Too Much and Didn't Go Up

If you're watching, you may see this on the final prove and can take corrective action then by re-kneading and tightening the dough with a little extra flour.

Under kneading or under developing the dough. The dough doesn't develop properly. Since the framework of gluten and gas isn't present, the cells can't do their job and the dough just spreads out. You can take this dough, knead it a bit and set it to rise again, giving it a shortened final rise time.

Over-proving, leaving the dough too long in the final rise. The dough structure begins to break down, so the dough just spreads out. With over-proved dough, you can try to reclaim by kneading very briefly and then setting the dough out for a short rise period. Doesn't always work, but worth a try.

A wet dough is very prone to this flaw, since the gluten structure is fairly delicate and easily deflated. Here, the fault may be a combination of under-development and over-proving.

As a novice you may find that no matter what you do, some wet doughs just don't work for you as free-standing loaves. No harm done. Get a tin of some sort and use that instead!

Help! My Crust is Too Dark

The most common cause of an overly-dark crust is simply baking too long, which will also result in a thicker crust. Some breads require a dark crust and some bakers like a darker crust. It will eat fine anyway, adjust the time next time so the crust is to your liking. If it's too crunchy for you, a tea towel over the loaf whilst it's cooling will trap the steam and soften the crust.

Oven temperature too high. Check the temperature before you start to bake. If you consistently have a dark crust, check your oven temperature with an oven thermometer.

If the crust is too dark on the top only, you may have set the oven shelf too close to the top of the oven. Simply lower it for next time.

If the crust is too dark on the bottom only, you may have the shelf too close to the bottom of the oven. Simply move it up for next time.

If you check the loaf when it is half-way baked and the top is already turning dark, you can slow the coloring by covering it with tin foil for the remainder of baking. Bread is not like cake, so you can check on its progress without detriment.

If you check the loaf when it is half-way baked and the bottom crust is getting very dark, you can slide a cold cooking sheet under the loaf and transfer the loaf to a higher rack in the oven.

Help! My Crust is Too Pale

Instead of a dark crust, you end up with a loaf the color of straw. Mostly it will be the reverse of the overly-dark crust, so the oven temperature was too low. Always check.

If you let the dough rise in a very warm place, it sometimes accelerates the dough activity enough to make it seem as if it is very old dough and then the browning reaction won't occur. Make sure you don't let your doughs rise in anything above 25°C. An ambient temperature of 20°C may slow the process down a wee bit, but will avoid some pitfalls.

The dough crust dried out during rising. In effect, there isn't enough moisture in the crust for the browning reaction, so the crust stays pale. Always cover a rising dough so it doesn't dry out.

Help! I've Got a Gap Between the Crust and the Rest of the Bread

In the trade this is called 'flying crust'. Some professional loaves have this flaw, so ignore it and call yourself a pro. If it bothers you, here are some possible causes:

The dough was allowed to rise for too long in a very dry environment. This is the primary cause. You can spritz the atmosphere with water from a spray bottle if you suffer from a very dry environment.

The final rise period was too short. This is not common, but it does sometimes happen. Just make sure you rise the dough for the proper amount of time.

Help! I've Got Streaks in my Bread

This is usually flour that got added during kneading or shaping. The flour gets into the dough but then doesn't get properly mixed, so it sits in the dough as raw flour. The way to avoid this fault is to refrain from adding extra flour during the last stages of kneading.

Help! The Holes in My Bread are Too Big

In some breads such as sourdough this wouldn't be a fault, but in your average sandwich loaf, it could be an issue.

The usual cause is over-proving of a wettish dough. If you look at properly made bread, you may notice that the texture of the loaf changes a bit from top to bottom. With larger holes toward the top and smaller holes towards the bottom. This is simply the weight of the dough squeezing the holes near the bottom while the holes near the top have little pressing down on them.

When the dough is allowed to rise for too long, the difference becomes more pronounced. Avoid this by allowing the dough to rise for only the time suggested in the recipe.

Over-proving can also occur if the temperature is too high in the area where the dough is rising. Make sure that the combination of time and temperature is correct.

At the end of the day

These are some of the possible problems and their causes, either alone or in combination. Because there are so many different causes and they can work together to foil your best efforts, the answers are often a combination of a few minor changes. The bottom line is that temperature and moisture levels do affect bread and sometimes you won't know what went wrong.

I nearly threw my bread maker out when I had a series of failed loaves until I worked out it was a bad batch of flour with very low gluten levels! Follow the recipes exactly. Measure and check everything, including your oven, and more often than not you'll turn out decent, edible bread.

When things go well, see if you can work out what you did correctly and you might avoid the mistakes of 'failed' loaves next time.

Soups and Lunches

Grated Beetroot and Vegetable Soup
Miso Broth
Veg Patch Minestrone
Lemony Lentil Soup
Cucumber and Pea Gazpacho
Scottish Onion Soup
Big Bowl Laksa
Store Cupboard Fishcakes
Leftovers Frittata
Store Cupboard Pasta Salad
Lentil Tabbouleh
Dhal and Rice
Crunchy Winter Salad
Roast Vegetable Wraps

I have the privilege and challenge of working from home. I can easily knock up a soup or a salad, or more often a weird combination from what's in the fridge, for my midday repast, even if it is at two in the afternoon.

I spent most of my working life in offices though and understand the challenges of eating something other than a hastily grabbed, speedily eaten sandwich. We all know eating at our desk is not a great idea and yet we often succumb to the pressure to do it.

Try and break the habit, at least a couple of times a week. Move about, grab a breath of fresh air, meet a friend and try some of these lunch suggestions. I promise you'll feel better for it.

The recipes can be made the night before or even in the morning if you're an early riser. The soups can be made at any time and frozen in portions sizes for you to reheat in the office microwave.

Grated Beetroot & Vegetable Soup

I could be trendy and call it Borscht, but I've been making this soup for decades and, well, it isn't really Borscht. It is itself: pretty, tasty, and importantly, very easy. It's one of our favourites here at HHC HQ. It makes a thin'ish soup with lots of vegetable matter. If you prefer a thicker soup, blitz half with a handheld stick blender and mix it back into the un-blended half. Whatever you do, don't make it smooth though, as the texture in this soup is part of its charm. I've stated quantities, but to be honest it doesn't much matter about being precise, as long as the beetroot are your star performers. If I have some spare red cabbage knocking about, I'll often add that too. The choice is yours.

Ingredients

2 large beetroot or around 350g
2 medium carrots or around 200g
1 large onion
1 garlic clove (optional)
1 tbsp tomato puree
1 tbsp tamari (or soy sauce*)

A couple of shakes of Worcestershire sauce
2 tsp balsamic vinegar
bay leaf
fresh ground black pepper
salt to taste
800ml vegetable stock

Method

Grate the vegetables in a processor, in batches, or by hand.

Add the grated veg to a large pan and add the vegetable stock. Add the tomato puree and other seasoning ingredients.

Bring to a slow simmer and cook for around 45 minutes, or until the vegetables are soft and all the vegetables and seasoning have amalgamated.

If you're intending to blitz half, do it now, removing the bay leaf first, then add the smooth soup back to the pan.

I like to serve this with plenty of pepper to offset the sweetness and some sour cream works well if you have it but it is by no means necessary. A cheese scone, turmeric bread or soda bread also work nicely to bolster lunch.

* Won't be GF if you use soy sauce; tamari is GF.

Soups and Lunches

Grated Beetroot & Vegetable Soup

Miso Broth

I confess this is barely a recipe. It gets knocked up when there's nothing much in the fridge and can be made with store cupboard ingredients if you have nothing else. It's salty and savoury and fits the bill for a quick lunch very nicely. Don't use a stock cube or the broth may be too salty. Save some water you've cooked vegetables in, if you don't have stock, or use water and adjust seasoning to taste. It's not especially beautiful to look at, but don't let that deter you. It's important not to boil this soup as it ruins the properties of the miso.

Ingredients

2 tbsp Miso* - any type will do, mixed with a little water
500ml vegetable stock
1 thumb-sized piece of ginger
2 garlic cloves
6 scallions (spring onions)
scattering of coriander leaf
¼ carrot, very finely sliced
1 chilli if you like a bit of heat

If you have them, you can add some thinly sliced fresh mushrooms, or some dried mushrooms, once they've been soaked and de-gritted.

Method

Finely slice the spring onions (scallions), ginger ,garlic and chilli, if using. Put the stock in a pot and add the veg. You can add the fresh sliced mushrooms (or dried mushrooms if you have them) at this stage too. Simmer gently, without boiling, for around 10 minutes. Add the miso and stir through. Scatter with the coriander and serve in mugs.

* If you don't keep miso in stock, you can buy packet/sachets of miso soup mix in boxes as either a dried mix or a paste. Use 2 sachets in place of the miso.

Top Tip

If you have a bit more time and wish to make this a heartier soup, you can add add 100g of noodles and some cubed tofu to the soup and cook through.

Vegetable Patch Minestrone

Minestrone soup is one of those soups that can be a delight or a poor excuse for the name of soup. In Italy I have had versions with rice, with pasta, with potatoes and with none of the above. What I have never had is a meat soup, or a tomato soup. This is peasant fare, and keeping to its roots makes it a better soup as far as I'm concerned. For me an authentic minestrone contains the vegetables of the season; it's made with a stock base and often includes tomatoes. I like to make it in the summer when beans, peas and fresh tomatoes are in abundance in the garden, hence the 'veg patch' moniker. The recipe is not prescriptive - make it with what you have.

Ingredients

1 onion diced
1 stick celery diced
2 carrots diced
1 courgette diced
50g green beans
50g frozen peas, or podded fresh peas if you can get them
100g of cooked cannellini beans, or half a can
2 large tomatoes or a tin of Italian plum tomatoes, chopped, if you don't have fresh

100g spinach, chard or cabbage finely chopped
50g pasta, for example macaroni
2 garlic cloves chopped
800ml stock
freshly ground black pepper - I like a lot and some versions I've eaten use this to add heat
handful of fresh parsley, stalks and leaves chopped separately.
handful fresh basil, torn or shredded
50g grated Parmesan (optional)

Method

Put two tablespoons of olive oil into a large saucepan or stock pot, add the onion and parsley stalks and sweat for about 5 minutes without browning. Add the celery and carrots and stir around for another few minutes. Add the stock and bring to a simmer.

Next add the cannellini beans, garlic and tomatoes. Cook for 30 minutes. Now add the potato and courgette and cook on a gentle simmer for another 30 minutes. Add the pepper and pasta and cook until al dente. Add the fresh herbs, check the seasoning and serve, removing the parmesan crust if you added it (see tip). If you like, grate fresh Parmesan on top.

Top Tip

If you're absolutely desperate to make this a meat soup, add some diced pancetta after you've sweated down the onion a bit.

If you have a bit of Parmesan 'crust' you can add this to the pot for the time it takes for the soup to cook. Remove before serving.

Soups and Lunches

Lemony Lentil Soup

Next to the Miso Broth, this is the easiest soup going. Three main ingredients, a few spices and you have something deliciously tasty. Lentils don't require overnight soaking, so just give them a few rinses and you're away.

Ingredients

1 onion, diced
2 cloves of garlic, finely chopped
250g red lentils
1.5L vegetable stock
½ tsp.turmeric
½ tsp ground cumin
1 bay leaf
handful of chopped coriander
zest and juice of half a lemon

Method

Heat the oil in a pan and gently fry the chopped onions until soft - about 5 minutes.

Add the garlic, bay leaf, spices and zested lemon rind and cook for a few minutes more.

Stir in the rinsed lentils, add the stock and cook for 25-35 minutes, until the lentils have broken down.

Stir several times during cooking, especially towards the end, to stop the lentils sticking to the base of the pan.

Stir in the coriander and lemon juice and leave to cook for a few more minutes.

If you want a really smooth soup, you can go to the trouble of blending it, but I generally prefer a bit of texture.

Top Tip

If you have bit more time and want to do something more with this simple recipe you can fry finely sliced onion until browned and top the soup with it.

Soups and Lunches

Cucumber & Pea Gazpacho

As is often the case with cooks who also garden, many recipes are the result of using up gluts - an excess of a particular crop. Last year we had more cucumbers than we could use and this chilled summer soup was the result. A Gazpacho is a cold soup of blended vegetables. The original Spanish version is an Andalusian classic. Whilst this soup may not reach such dizzying heights, I hope you will find it tasty enough to make it part of your summer repertoire. You could use courgettes instead of the cucumber if you have a glut of those. Lightly cook them first and cool if you don't like the taste of raw courgette.

Ingredients

2 small cucumbers (or 1 large)
a handful of lettuce,
a few sprigs of watercress
6 little tomatoes
1 stick of celery
6 spring onions
4 tbsp peas

basil, mint & parsley (reserve some for decoration)
200ml cooled vegetable stock
half cap of red wine vinegar
a few drops of hot chilli sauce
sea salt and freshly ground black pepper
2 tbsp olive oil, for serving

Method

Reserve a couple of the tomatoes, and a couple of tbsp of the other veg, all finely chopped, keep a spoonful of the peas whole.

Chop the rest of the veg into chunks and slices and put everything into a high-speed blender or liquidiser. Add the seasoning ingredients, herbs, stock and one tbsp olive oil.

Blend on high power until everything is blended as you like. Check the seasoning and leave for a couple of hours for the flavours to mingle. The soup can be left overnight in the fridge, but take it out to reach room temperature before serving.

When you're ready to serve the soup, tip into 2 bowls and spoon the reserved chopped vegetables on top. Drizzle with olive oil and garnish with some torn herb leaves.

Top Tip

If you have some spare day-old bread, you can make croutons.

Use 3 thick slices bread from whatever bread you have to hand. Heat the oven to 180C/160C Fan/Gas 4. Cut the bread into rough cubes, toss the bread in the oil and sprinkle with salt. Scatter the pieces on to an oven tray and bake for 8-10 mins or until the croutons are browned and crunchy. Put on a timer so you don't forget them as they burn easily!

Soups and Lunches

Scottish Onion Soup

I love the classic French onion soup but don't have the patience to wait until the onions caramelise. I've developed this alternative version instead, which makes the best of Scottish produce, and has the advantage of being on the table in less time!

Ingredients

6 large onions, cut in half and finely sliced
300g leeks, trimmed, washed and sliced
2L organic vegetable stock
Worcestershire sauce
cider vinegar
1 tsp mustard of your choice (optional)
a few fresh sage leaves finely chopped

knob of butter
sea salt and freshly ground black pepper

For the crouts (optional):
8 slices good-quality day old bread
150g Scottish Cheddar cheese, freshly grated

Method

Put the butter and a generous amount of olive oil in a large heavy-based pan and heat until the butter melts. Add the sliced onions and cover with a spare butter paper or a piece of baking parchment. Cook on a low heat for 10-15 minutes until soft, but do not allow to brown.

Add the sliced leeks and a glug more oil if required, and cook on a low heat until the leeks are softening and the onions are beginning to take on some colour.

Stir occasionally to prevent sticking.

When your onions and leeks are lovely and soft (20-25 minutes), add the stock, vinegar, and Worcestershire sauce. Bring up to a boil then turn the heat down and simmer for 10-15 minutes.

Season the soup and add the mustard. In a ramekin dish, mix a teaspoon of mustard with a little of the hot soup, then add to the rest of the soup and stir again.

Serve with a few sage leaves for adornment.

If you're planning on making crouts to top the soup with, use this time to preheat the grill to high and then toast your bread on both sides.

Ladle the soup into heatproof bowls and then put the toasted bread over each bowl. Sprinkle with some grated Cheddar.

Put the bowls on a baking tray under the grill to melt the cheese. Allow to golden if you prefer it that way.

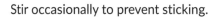
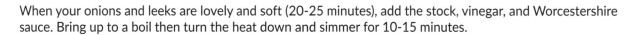

Soups and Lunches

Big Bowl Laksa

This is hearty fare for cold days and hungry people. Although there are a lot of ingredients, it doesn't take much to get this steaming bowl of loveliness on the table, and as an added bonus it can be made in 30 minutes or less.

Serves 4 - 6 depending on the level of greed!

Ingredients

1 pack of firm Tofu (marinated or smoked)
4 spring onions, chopped
1 fresh red chilli,
3 garlic cloves
1 tbsp freshly grated root ginger
1 tbsp ground turmeric
1 tbsp peanut butter
2 tbsp tamari (or soy sauce*)
1 tbsp sesame oil
2 tbsp vegetable oil
400ml coconut milk
1 litre vegetable stock
pack of rice noodles

100g bean sprouts
100g beans or asparagus or veg of choice
100g butternut squash cubed

To serve:
fresh mint leaves
fresh coriander leaves
4 lime wedges
2 tbsp peanuts, roughly chopped or sesame seeds (optional)
2 tbsp Sriracha hot sauce (or use a hot chilli sauce, but not a sweet one) or fresh chilli if you're brave.

Method

To make the laksa paste, put the spring onions, chilli, garlic, ginger, turmeric, peanut butter, tamari (or soy sauce*) and sesame oil in a small food processor and blend until smooth. Scrape down the sides. Add a little of the stock if it's too sticky to blitz.

Heat the vegetable oil over a medium heat in a large pan or wok. Cook the laska paste for 2 minutes or until you can smell the garlic beginning to cook. Stir in the coconut milk and vegetable stock, then bring to a simmer.

Stir in the tofu and butternut squash. Reduce the heat to medium and cook for 10-15 minutes or until the squash is tender and the tofu is heated through. Be careful not to break up the tofu.

Stir in the bean sprouts and green veg (or veg of your choice) and noodles and cook for 2-3 minutes or until vegetables are just tender and the noodles "al dente".

Divide among the bowls. Top with mint, coriander and peanuts (or sesame seeds), drizzle with the chillis, or Sriracha sauce, and serve with lime wedges.

* Won't be GF if you use soy sauce; tamari is GF.

Soups and Lunches

Store Cupboard Fishcakes

Don't knock them until you've tried them. These taste a lot better than many fishcakes I've had out and have the advantage of being cheap and easy to rustle up in a hurry. I often make extra mash so I can make them.

Ingredients

250g cold, cooked, floury potato
125g tin fish in oil or water, drained
a bunch of spring onions, finely sliced (or a medium onion finely chopped)
1 tbsp capers, roughly chopped if large
1 medium egg
rapeseed or sunflower oil, for cooking
4 tbsp fine polenta or maize meal, for coating

Method

Mash the cooked potatoes roughly.

Put the drained tinned fish in a bowl and mash with a fork to break it up a little. Add the onion, capers, mashed potato and some black pepper. Lightly beat the egg and add this too. Stir the ingredients together.

Divide the mixture into four. Roll each portion into a ball, then squash lightly into a cake. At this stage you can chill them to firm them up if you have the time and inclination. If not, heat a non-stick frying pan covered with a thin coating of oil over a medium heat.

Put the polenta in a bowl and season well with salt and pepper. Carefully transfer one of the fishcakes to the bowl of polenta and coat it all over, then gently place in the pan. Repeat with the rest. If you've not chilled them, do handle gently as they have a tendency to break up if you don't.

Cook for about 15 minutes, turning once or twice, until the coating is crisp and golden and the cakes are heated through.

Soups and Lunches

Leftovers Frittata

This is fast food at its best, made even better by the virtue of using up whatever you may have leftover or lurking in the fridge. Use whatever you have to hand, but make sure the veg are cooked and cooled before you add them to the egg mixture. Seasoning and cooking are key to avoid a bland mess of eggs and veg. Make sure you use plenty of freshly ground pepper and a generous dose of sea salt. If you have herbs, all the better. Parsley, thyme, sage, rosemary and oregano all work well. Use a heavy-based pan that will fit into your oven, as frittatas cook best if you use a mixture of stove top and grill or oven cooking. If you have some old cheese hanging about in the fridge - Parmesan, Feta, Gruyere or Cheddar - feel free to add that too. This is not an 'everything but the kitchen sink' recipe however, so choose a handful of things you like and have about, rather than seeing how much you can cram in. You will turn out a lunch that you can serve hot to guests, or cool to take to work as your packed lunch.

Ingredients

6 eggs
leftover veg, for example:
broccoli,
potatoes,
courgette
peppers

peas
onions, cooked
use whatever you like and have to hand.
fresh herbs
cheese (optional)

Method

Preheat your grill to medium-high.

Chop your leftover veg, except the peas. I always add peas and onion even if they're not 'leftovers' as they add colour and flavour to the finished dish.

Beat the eggs in a large jug as though you were making an omlette. Season well.

Heat the oil in your ovenproof frying pan or cast-iron skillet. Add the diced potatoes, onions, broccoli, peppers and courgette to heat through.

Mix the peas with the eggs, then pour over the veg in the pan. Give it a shoogle around to even out the vegetables. Add the herbs (and cheese, if you're using it) then cook until the base is firm. The top will still be liquidy.

Pop it under the grill until the cheese melts and the frittata is firm.

Alternatively you can put the frittata in the oven at 200C/180C Fan/Gas 6 for 15 minutes.

Top Tip

Serve with salad and good bread for a tasty main meal or with the homemade baked beans for a substantial breakfast.

Store Cupboard Pasta Salad

Now, I have to confess that I am not a fan of cold pasta. Hot, silky pasta with a clinging sauce, yes, but cold pasta salad, not so much. When faced with leftover pasta however, I rarely reheat it as it over-cooks. As I refuse to throw food away, this recipe was developed. I like it so much that I deliberately make extra pasta a couple of times during the summer so we can eat it as part of a picnic or on-the-patio lunch.

I like to use a coloured pasta such as beetroot or spinach as it makes the finished result more interesting, but anything you have - with the possible exception of spaghetti/tagliatelle - will be fine. The dressing is very punchy; feel free to adjust to your own taste.

Serves 2. Easily bulked up. 15 minutes.

Ingredients

150g leftover pasta
1 tbsp sundried tomatoes in oil
1 tbsp peppers in oil
1 tbsp good olives
I red onion, diced

For the dressing:
1 heaped tbsp capers, drained and chopped
2 anchovies, mashed to a paste

juice and zest of 1 lime
1 clove garlic, finely chopped
1 heaped tsp grainy mustard
2 tbsp fresh coriander leaves, chopped
2 tbsp fresh parsley, chopped
2 tbsp basil
3 tbsp extra virgin olive oil
Freshly milled black pepper

Method

First make the dressing by whisking together the capers, lime zest and juice, mustard, garlic, olive oil, anchovy and herbs.

Add your pasta shapes to another bowl and add all the other ingredients, except the seasoning and dressing.

Give the dressing another good whisk and pour over the pasta salad. Stir well. Check seasoning and adjust if necessary.

This is a versatile dish and you can basically add whatever you like that you can find in your fridge and store cupboard. Tinned fish works well to boost the protein profile. However, it's the punchy dressing that makes this dish work, so whatever you do, don't leave that out or you'll have a very second rate version.

Soups and Lunches

Lentil Tabbouleh

Tabbouleh is a simple Middle Eastern salad of very finely chopped vegetables, lots of fresh herbs and bulgur wheat, all tossed with citrus juice and olive oil. In this gluten-free version, I switch the wheat for puy lentils which makes for an easy and interesting substitute. It's easy to up the quantities and take it on a sharing picnic.

Ingredients

200g puy lentils
6 spring onions
1 pack cherry tomatoes
½ a cucumber
½ a small bunch of each of the following herbs:
mint
flat-leaf parsley
leaf coriander

For the dressing:
2 tbsp olive oil
1 lime, juiced

Method

Rinse the lentils, then cook in plenty of salted water until tender.

Drain and set aside to cool.

Trim and finely slice the spring onions, and quarter the cherry tomatoes.

Scrape the seeds out of the cucumber and finely dice.

Finely chop the herb leaves.

Mix the cooled lentils with the spring onions, tomatoes, cucumber and herbs.

Add the oil and lime juice and season with the sea salt and freshly ground black pepper.

Top Tip

Serve with feta or halloumi cheese to boost the protein content.

Soups and Lunches

GF

Dahl & Rice

There is a version of this dish in many cultures: Caribbean rice and peas, Cuban black beans and rice and many Middle Eastern Dishes which include anything from chickpeas to black beans. Most homes on the Indian sub-continent will have their own version of this dish which sustains a large proportion of households daily. You could do worse than add this cheap and nourishing dish to your repetoire.

I spent years trying to make a decent dhal. The secret is simplicity - my local Indian restaurant were kind enough to give me a steer: cook the dhal plain and add the spices to the finished dish.

Ingredients

400g red lentils, rinsed in a sieve under cold running water
½ onion, sliced
2 tsp ground turmeric
2 tsp cumin seeds
3 garlic cloves, finely chopped
1-2 green chillies, finely chopped, to taste
salt and pepper
1L water
1 bay leaf
15g butter

For the rice:
200g rice, cook according to the packet instructions. I use a lot of water rather than the absorption method, due to fears around arsenic. Use whichever method you prefer.
1 cinnamon stick   } Remove these
2 cardamon pods   } before serving
6 coriander seeds   }
Leaf coriander to garnish with the spices

Method

Place the lentils into a pan and cover with enough water to come a couple of cm above the lentils, depending on pan size. Bring to a boil, skimming off any froth as you go. Reduce the heat. Once simmering, add the turmeric and bay leaf.

Simmer gently for 15-20 minutes, or until the lentils are completely softened and the water is absorbed, but the mixture not dry.

Meanwhile, heat a small frying pan over a medium heat. Add the cumin seeds and dry fry until toasted and aromatic (about 1-2 minutes).

Top Tip

I often make a double batch of the lentils and freeze it to make another dahl, but you can also use it to make lentil patties if you make it a little thicker. It thickens as it cools.

Remove the cumin seeds from the pan and set to one side. Add 2 tablespoons of oil to the pan and fry the onion until it is starting to brown. Add the garlic and chopped green chilli and fry for 1-2 minutes, or until the garlic turns light golden-brown, and the chilli is softened. Add the toasted cumin seeds back to the pan and remove from the heat.

Once the lentils are soft, give them a vigorous stir to break them up a little. Stir the onion, garlic, spice mixture and any oil into the the lentils and mix well. Taste and adjust the seasoning as necessary. Stir in the knob of butter.

Serve the dahl alongside the cooked rice garnished with the coriander. If you want to incorporate some additional protein, some fried eggs, chicken or fish would go well, although this is a substantial dish and perfectly good on its own.

Soups and Lunches

Crunchy Winter Salad

This is a pimped up winter slaw, with a punchy dressing in place of a mayonnaise. We make a big batch over Christmas and serve it with all manner of festive delights: cold cuts, pork pie, vegetable jalousie. It is equally at home on a jacket potato for lunch or as part of a pick'n'mix salad in your lunch box. You can switch mayo for the dressing, but give the dressing a try first and see what you think.

Ingredients

200g carrots
¼ red cabbage
½ small celeriac
1 red onion
50g sunflower and pumpkin seeds

For the dressing:
50g raisins
2 tbsp red wine vinegar
1 tsp Dijon mustard
4 tbsp olive oil

Method

Peel the carrots and celeriac and grate in a food processor, a mandolin or by hand, depending on what you prefer and the level of thickness you like.

Thinly slice the red cabbage. Mix everything together, except the dressing.

Whisk the oil and vinegar with some mustard, salt and pepper and toss with the salad immediately to stop the celeriac going brown.

Refrigerate, covered, to store.

Roast Vegetable Wraps

This is a versatile recipe. You can make it from leftover roast veggies – from the polenta and roast veg on page 95, for example, or you can make up a batch specially. You can use the flatbread recipe on page 40 if you fancy having a go at making some wraps yourself. Otherwise use shop bought tortilla. You can add pesto, hummus or salad to your wraps, but the veg alone is an ample and tasty lunch.

Ingredients
1 red pepper, sliced
1 yellow pepper, sliced
200g portabello mushroom sliced
1 red onion, sliced
2 cloves garlic, crushed or grated
1 tbsp balsamic vinegar
1 tbsp olive oil
sea salt and freshly ground black pepper
fresh herbs such as parsley, coriander or oregano
8 cherry tomatoes (cut into halves)
feta cheese (optional)
pesto, hummus or kiwi salsa sauce (optional) - See 'Snacks, Sides and Sauces' chapter for recipes
2 flour tortilla/wraps or a couple of flat breads if you have them

Method
Preheat oven to 200C/180C Fan/Gas6. In a large bowl, toss mushrooms, peppers, onions and garlic with olive oil and balsamic vinegar.

Spread on baking sheet, so you have one layer, and season.

Roast in the oven for approximately 25 minutes or until the vegetables are softening and starting to brown. Add the tomatoes and cook for 10 minutes more. Allow to cool then and add the herbs of your choice.

Spoon roasted vegetables in centre of a wrap, spoon on the pesto, hummus or salsa, and/or crumble the feta over, if using.

Tuck both sides in and roll the wrap. You can cut them before you eat them, but they travel best whole.

Easy to make the night before for a tasty packed lunch. Take the pesto or hummus with you, if using, as it will make the wrap very soggy if you add it the previous evening.

Soups and Lunches

Roast Vegetable Wraps

Main Meals

Seedy Herby Pudding
Savoury Vegetable Rice
The Ultimate Chilli Con Carne
Vegetable Chilli
Pasta al Pomodoro
Black Bean Burgers
Pea Cakes with Poached Eggs
Roasted Veggies with Soft Polenta
HHC Veggie Haggis
Shepherdess Pie
Prawn Curry
Chicken Curry

People eat their main meal of the day at different times.

These meals are suitable for any time of day, and could be eaten as a lunch or dinner. I try to eat three meals of a similar size throughout the day, rather than a large meal later in the evening, although I appreciate that circumstances often dictate when you eat. Try not to let that dictate what you eat too often though.

These meals are suitable for mid-week meals or something a bit more time consuming at the weekend. The guide times for some of the meals may seem excessive, but rest assured this usually represents cooking time rather than actual preparation time. Some meals can be on the table in a little over half an hour, the others can be made in advanced and reheated.

Seedy Herby Pudding

OK, I'll confess. This started life as a stuffing recipe. When I was 11, I embarked on my vegetarian journey. There were no vegetarian foods available in the supermarket, and vegetarians were treated with a degree of suspicion, as if not eating meat was a highly dubious lifestyle choice. My Mum was convinced I would fade away from malnutrition. So began a lifetime of inventing recipes. This is the first truly edible thing I made, and I still favour it now as a Sunday lunch, in preference to a factory-made nut loaf, or similar offering. It is tasty and you can pimp it up as much as you like.

As it stands, it will easily serve 4. If you choose to add sausage meat, for example, as a non-vegetarian version, it will obviously serve more. To bulk it up and keep it veggie, chestnuts and/or mushrooms are a good choice.

Ingredients

1 onion, finely diced
25g butter
300g fresh wholemeal breadcrumbs
150g seeds: 60g sunflower, 60g pumpkin & 30g sesame; half blitzed, half left whole
a fistful of fresh herbs, chopped: rosemary, sage, parsley & thyme
1 free range organic egg, beaten
sea salt, freshly ground black pepper
600ml water

Method

Place a pot on with enough water to cover the chopped onion. Add the chopped herbs and cook until the onion is softened (about 15-20 minutes).

Add the breadcrumbs and seeds to the onions, and mix well. Remove from the heat and allow to cool slightly. Add the beaten egg, the butter and season well. If the mixture seems too dry, add a splash of water. It should be thick, but not too stiff or it will dry out too much in the oven.

Transfer the pudding mix to a buttered 1lb loaf tin or ovenproof dish. Place this on an oven tray and cook covered (I use a butter paper) in the oven at 200C/Fan 180C/Gas 6 for 25-30 minutes. Remove the butter paper and allow to brown for a further 10 minutes.

If you want to slice the pudding, allow to cool slightly to firm up, otherwise, serve from the tin in spoonfuls.

We have this with roast potatoes and lots of veg for a tasty and filling Sunday lunch. Feel free to serve it as a 'stuffing' for a meat meal if you must. It won't disappoint.

Main Meals

Savoury Vegetable Rice

OK. I know it's only rice and vegetables. I know you can probably buy it ready made, but this is a simple recipe that can be served as a main meal for the vegetarians in your life, or as a side dish instead of your usual carb choices.

It's easy to increase the quantities if you have unexpected guests and it can be on the table within half and hour. It's also very easy to pimp up with different herbs and spices - I often use ginger and leaf coriander - as well as adding protein elements: tofu, prawns or chicken, for example.

This is not a risotto, so there's no stirring involved. You'll end up with separate grains of rice, jewelled with vegetables. Don't overcook the rice or you'll end up with a stodgy mess!

Ingredients

150g brown Basmati rice
1 red onion, chopped
1 stalk celery chopped
100g mushrooms, sliced
½ red pepper, diced
50g peas
1 tbsp vegetable oil
1 garlic clove grated or crushed
1 tomato chopped
1 tsp garam masala
1 tsp vegetable stock powder dissolved in 550ml boiling water
3 tbsp chopped fresh parsley or a few basil leaves to garnish

Method

Heat 1 tablespoon of vegetable oil in a pan over medium heat; add onion and fry until soft add the garlic and fry for a minute without browning.

Add the celery, mushrooms and red pepper; cook for a further 5 minutes.

Stir in the rice. Add the stock, peas and garam masala.

Simmer for 15 minutes, or until the rice is tender. Stir in the chopped tomato.

Serve the rice topped with chopped parsley or torn basil leaves.

Season to taste.

Top Tip

If you want to bulk up the dish or add to the protein content, you can add a handful of cashew nuts along with the vegetables. You can also top this with a cheese, such as feta, after serving.

The Ultimate Chilli Con Carne

This is my 'go to' version of this classic dish and people have often asked for the recipe, so here it is. This is the sort of recipe you need up your sleeve when friends and family come to call. It serves 6 hungry people, or more, if you accompany it with rice, avocado, spring onions and tacos. I never make any less as it freezes well for a handy standby meal or two. Make it a day ahead and the flavours will meld together and the meat will be meltingly tender.

You can use minced beef, rather than steak, if you prefer, or your budget is tight; although the economy mince is rarely worth it as you'll be draining off a ton of fat. Browning meat is a bit of a faff and can be time consuming. It is worth the effort, believe me. If you leave out this stage it will be a very different dish. Feel free to vary herbs and leave out the wine, if you don't drink alcohol. Add an extra splash of wine vinegar and make up the liquid with stock. If, like me, you're not a chilli head, you can reduce the amount of chilli and still have a warming, vibrant dish.

Ingredients

1200 skirt steaks or lean stewing beef
75g diced pancetta or rashers of rindless smoked streaky bacon
2 tbsp olive oil
2 onions, chopped
4 garlic cloves, finely chopped
1 unwaxed lemon or preserved lemon if you have one
1 small red or green chilli
1 carrot, grated
1 celery stick, finely chopped
3 tbsp Mexican chilli powder

1 tbsp smoked paprika
1 tsp ground cumin
1 tbsp flour
2 bay leaves
2 tsp dried oregano
1 tbsp red wine vinegar
2 tbsp tomato purée
A single cube of dark chocolate
300ml red wine
200ml beef stock
1 x 400g tin of Italian tomatoes
2 x 400g tin black beans, drained

Method

Cut all the meat into small chunks. In a spacious, heavy-based pan, fry the pancetta in the oil over a medium heat until it is crisp and the fat has melted.

Stir the onions, garlic, carrot and celery into the crisping pancetta and cook, stirring often, for 10-15 mins until soft.

Cut the lemon into quarters lengthways, then remove the pithy core and seeds. Chop into small pieces (each with a bit of peel). Remove the pan from the heat and scoop the contents into a sieve, letting any fat drain back into the pan. Use a wooden spoon to encourage the oil back to the pan if necessary.

Return the pan to the heat and brown the steak or mince in batches in the hot fat. If there's a lot of fat left in the pan when you've finished frying the meat, tip all but a tablespoon out.

Add the chilli powder and cumin, and cook over a low heat for 2 mins, stirring constantly. Add the flour and cook for a further 2 mins. Add the bay leaves, ½ tsp salt, the lemon, oregano, tomato purée, red wine, if using, tomatoes and stock.

Return the onions, garlic and pancetta to the pan.

Bring to a simmer, stirring often, then reduce the heat and cook, uncovered, and stirring occasionally to avoid sticking, for 1½ hrs until the sauce is thick and the liquid has reduced.

Add the chocolate and beans to the chilli and cook for a further ½ hour. Add salt to taste.

I often cook this the day before I use it and add an extra tin of tomatoes. If you do this, make sure you cook it for long enough that the flavours amalgamate properly with the dish.

Serve with rice and accompaniments such as diced avocado, sliced spring onions and sour cream.

Top Tip

Browning meat is a bit of a faff and can be time consuming.

It is worth it. Do it in small batches in a heavy-based or non-stick pan so it doesn't boil.

Vegetable Chilli

This is the chilli recipe I've been using for four decades. Always a very popular dish. You can adjust the vegetables depending on the season. I always use mushrooms for texture, but in summer I swap the squash for courgettes.

Ingredients

1 onion, chopped
2 fat cloves of garlic chopped or crushed
1 green chilli, chopped
300g mushrooms, sliced or quartered, if large
300g butternut squash, roasted and cut into chunks
1 celery sticks, finely chopped
1 sweet pepper (red, yellow or orange), finely chopped
2 tsp chipotle paste. Use chilli powder to taste if you don't have this
2 tbsp red wine vinegar

1 square dark chocolate (70% cocoa solid minimum or a tsp unsweetened cocoa powder)
1 tbsp dried oregano
1 tbsp sweet smoked paprika
1 tbsp tomato paste
1 tbsp ground cumin
1 tsp ground cinnamon
2 x 400g cans chopped tomatoes
1 x 400g cans black beans, drained and rinsed
sea salt and freshly ground black pepper

To serve: chopped, fresh parsley.

Method

First, heat the oven to 200C/180C Fan/Gas 6. Cut the squash in half, season and oil lightly. Place cut side down and roast for 25-30 minutes or until a knife goes through easily. Place to one side and peel, chop when cool enough to handle.

Meanwhile put the onions, celery and chopped peppers with the oil in a large, heavy-based saucepan, and fry gently over a low heat until soft but not coloured. Add the chilli and garlic.

Next add the tinned tomatoes. Add the chipotle paste, tomato paste, oregano, paprika, cumin, cinnamon, vinegar and chocolate. Stir everything together. Top one of the empty tomato cans with water and add this. Bring to a simmer and cook gently for half an hour. Add the mushrooms and squash and beans and cook for a further 20 minutes, stirring occasionally. Season to taste, adding extra chilli if you enjoy it especially hot.

Serve with spring onions, and sour cream, tacos and/or rice and diced avocado if you like.

It's easy to scale up this recipe, but you'll need a very large pan, or to split it between two pans. Store in the freezer for an easy sharing meal.

Main Meals

4-6

1 hour

GF

Pasta Al Pomodoro

This classic tomato and pasta dish, probably the first one we all made, is easily overlooked. Get it right and it's a quick, stunning and satisfying dish. Unfortunately, it is often done badly, especially in chain restaurants. Recover the joy and master this classic yourself. You won't regret it.

With a classic Italian sauce in your repertoire, you have many more dishes at your fingertips: pimped with chilli and you have Arrabiata, add some salty olives, anchovies and capers and you have Puttenesca.

This recipe makes quite a bit of sauce so you may not want to use it all. Freeze it if you decide to keep some back.

Ingredients

1kg fresh ripe tomatoes in summer. Cut a slit in the tomatoes, but keep them whole (use tinned any time of year: 2 tins of Italian plum tomatoes).
1 onion
1 clove of garlic
1 tsp red wine vinegar
fresh black pepper and sea salt to taste
400g pasta - spaghetti is the classic pasta for this sauce

Method

Sweat the chopped onion in a little olive oil until translucent, then add the tomatoes. and place them in a pan with the chopped onion and a little salt. Crush them a little with a wooden spoon then cook uncovered on a medium heat for 15-20 minutes. Do not boil.

Blitz with a hand blender, mouli legume or liquidiser.

Put the sauce back on a slow heat adding the vinegar. Cook until thickened, and all the watery content has evaporated - about 20 minutes.

Check and adjust the seasoning. The sauce will 'hold' until the spaghetti is cooked. Cook according to packet instructions until "al dente" - cooked but with a little bite. I usually scoop the pasta into the sauce with a spaghetti spoon, to combine and serve, but if you're happier draining it, then do that.

Serve with Parmesan and basil.

Black Bean Burgers

You can use any pulses to make this recipe, but I like the colour and texture of black beans.

I first ate something similar in Cranks restaurant in London in the eighties, and so began my love affair with beans, lentils and pulses.

This makes a very satisfying pattie, whether you're a meat or vegetable eater.

Ingredients

400g can black beans
1 red onion, finely chopped
1 garlic clove, crushes
2 tbsps fresh corinader leaf
100g chestnut mushrooms, sliced and fried in olive oil

1 tsp tamari (or soy sauce*)
1 tsp chilli sauce (not the sweet kind)
sea salt and freshly ground pepper to taste

Method

Mash the beans, then add the other ingredients, including the cooked mushrooms. You can lightly blitz the mixture if you prefer, but I like to leave some texture in it. I usually chill the mixture before making it into patties, but it isn't strictly necessary.

Shape the mixture into 4 balls and flatten into patties, or make 2 large ones if you prefer. Fry until crisp and brown on one side (about 6-8 minutes) then carefully turn and brown on the other side. Don't push them around the pan too much, or they'll tend to break up.

Serve with burger trimmings such as mayo, tomato, salad, gherkins, etc. or any of the "sides" such as wedges or winter coleslaw.

* Won't be GF if you use Soy Sauce; Tamari is GF.

Main Meals

Pea Cakes with Poached Eggs

This is definitely a case of 'necessity being the mother of invention'. As with the porridge pancake recipe this was devised as a result of leftover mushy peas. I appreciate these may not be something everyone loves as much as I do, so if you don't have dried marrowfat peas, you can use a tin of 'mushy peas' but you may need to add a little flour to the mix as they'll be too wet to form cakes. Even if you don't like mushy peas, give these a try - they're really good!

Ingredients

1 small onion or shallot, chopped
250g dried marrowfat peas
30g butter
50g fresh spinach, chopped
30g Parmesan, grated
2 tsp lemon juice
A couple of sprigs of fresh thyme (or 1tsp of dried)

For coating:
80g quick cook polenta
1 egg
Plus eggs for poaching

Method

If you don't have "leftover" mushy peas, cover the dried peas in water and cook until softened (45-60 mins). Ensure that they don't stick to the bottom of the pot. You may need to add a little more water as they cook down.

Put the cooled, cooked peas into a food processor with the onion (or shallot), butter, Parmesan, spinach, thyme, 1 egg, seasoning and lemon juice.

Blitz until combined, but not entirely smooth.

Chill in the fridge for an hour.

Shape into patties with your hands (if you wet your hands it stops the mix sticking) 2cm thick and 8cm across makes 4 – 5 substantial cakes. Make them smaller if you want more.

Beat the second egg and place in a flat dish. In a second flattish dish, plate or small food tray, place the polenta. Coat each cake, first with the egg and then the polenta.

Fry over a medium heat in olive oil for about 8 minutes, turning frequently so the polenta doesn't burn and the cakes heat through.

Serve warm with poached eggs on top.

Top Tip

Make extra pea cakes and freeze them! If you're doing this, freeze them once you've made and coated the patties. When you come to cook them, cook from frozen, turning often until hot all the way through.

Main Meals

Pea Cakes with Poached Eggs

Roasted Veggies with Soft Polenta

This is one of those really simple, but tasty and colourful dishes, that are great for a supper for two or a feast for many. Chopping a few veg and stirring the polenta is as much effort as is required. This is a 'summer' veg mix, for a winter mix, substitute with squash, celeriac and mushrooms.

To increase the protein content, crumble some feta over the veg, or add some sliced halloumi. For meat eaters you can easily roast some chicken at the same time as you cook the veg.

Ingredients

For the roasted veg:
1 aubergine, cut into chunks
2 mixed coloured peppers, cut into chunks
1 red onion, cut into wedges
2 courgettes, cut into chunks
200g cherry tomatoes
4 garlic cloves, smashed
3 sprigs of thyme, a sprig of rosemary and a handful of basil leaves
zest of 1 lemon

For the polenta:
100 ml milk (substitute with water if you like, it will make a slightly less creamy mixture)
600ml water
125g polenta grain/meal
35g Parmesan cheese

Method

For the roasted veg:
Heat the oven to 200C/180C Fan/Gas 6. Mix the oil with the aubergine, peppers, red onion, courgette, garlic, rosemary and thyme in a bowl with sea salt and black pepper. Tip onto a large roasting tray then roast for 30 mins. Or until softening and tinged with brown.

Whilst these are cooking make the polenta.

Add the tomatoes to the tin and return to the oven to continue cooking for a further 10 minutes.

Scatter over the basil and lemon zest, serve with the polenta.

For the polenta:
Pour the water into a large, heavy-based pan along with the milk (if using). Add a teaspoon of sea salt and bring it to the boil.

Pour in the polenta in a thin stream, stirring all the time so it thickens as you go. Keep whisking for 2-3 minutes over a medium-high heat.

Turn down the heat to the lowest setting and cook it for about 20 minutes, or according to the packet instructions. You are looking for the polenta to begin coming away from the pan. It gets really thick at this stage and starts bubbling like Vesuvius, even on a low heat, so stir every few minutes until cooked.

Add a little olive oil and stir in the Parmesan. Serve with the roasted veg.

Main Meals

Roasted Veggies with Soft Polenta

HHC Veggie Haggis

Highland Home Cook Veggie Haggis Makes 4 haggis bungs. Adjust according to requirement or make a batch and freeze.

This recipe is a 'trade secret'. No, really! I shouldn't be leaving it in a cookbook for all to see but so many people love my HHC haggis and have asked for the recipe that I had to include it. I'll trust you not to share my secrets with the world, or try and produce it commercially!

I make this recipe as both 'bungs' and slices. Cellulose bungs can be bought online, but if you don't want to go to the hassle - and it is a bit of a faff - then simply roll the mix into a very fat sausage shape, wrap in greaseproof, or similar, and chill for an hour.

Steam for 45mins or slice into rounds and fry.

Ingredients

250g pinhead oatmeal
100g red lentils
100g fresh wholemeal breadcrumbs
1 tin pinto beans, mashed
50g mixed nuts and/or seeds, ground
1 large onion, finely chopped
1 carrot
250g mushrooms chopped

600ml veg stock or stock cube and water
1 tsp yeast extract
1 tbsp lemon juice
tamari (or soy) sauce
Herbs spices and seasonings. Use any/all of the following in small quantities to your taste:
Sea salt, fresh ground black pepper, mace, nutmeg, paprika, bay leaf, rosemary, thyme, celery seeds.

Method

Heat some oil in a large pan and fry the onions, carrot and mushrooms for 5-10 mins until soft, add the lentils and half the oatmeal and ¾ of the stock and heat to simmering. Cook for 10 mins or until the lentils begin to soften. Add ½ the oatmeal and combine well.

In a bowl add the remainder of the stock to the mashed kidney beans along with the tamari, lemon juice, yeast extract, herbs and spices. Mix together and add to the pan.

Adjust seasoning and finally add the remaining breadcrumbs, nuts, oatmeal, salt and pepper, and mix well.

Cook for around 15-20 mins, adding more liquid or oatmeal as necessary to achieve the right consistency which should be stodgy and porridge like. Don't let it dry out too much or it will be very dry when you re cook it.

HHC Veggie Haggis

Shepherdess Pie

This is another of those recipes I hit on when I was exploring veggie food in the 70's. There were very few cookery books about and very little specialist food available, except in 'weird' wholefood shops that sold brown rice. We'd always had 'stew mix' at home and red lentils were also available in some places. I love their earthiness and versatility. They make a great base for a mashed potato top, cooked simply with onions and herbs. This is that original 1970's recipe and one I still use today.

Ingredients

1 onion, chopped
1 carrot, diced or grated
1 stick celery, chopped
1 garlic clove, finely chopped
50g chestnut mushrooms, chopped
200g red lentils, washed and drained
800ml vegetable stock
2 bay leaves
1 tbsp dried thyme

1 tbsp fresh chives
1 tbsp tomato puree

For the mash topping:
1kg floury potato
50g butter
50ml milk
30g mature cheddar, grated

Method

Heat oil in a large, heavy-based pan, then fry onions, diced carrots, celery and garlic cloves for around 10 mins until soft and golden.

Turn up the heat, add the diced chestnut mushrooms and cook for a further 5 minutes.

Stir in bay, thyme, then add the 200g lentils. Pour over the vegetable stock. Don't add salt yet as it makes the outer skin of the lentil tough and it takes longer to absorb the water. Simmer for 20-30 mins, until the lentils are very soft. Add extra liquid if it looks dry.

Season to taste, then stir in the tomato purée. remove from the heat and cool slightly, the mixture will thicken.

While the lentils are cooking, boil the potatoes for about 15 mins until cooked. Drain well, mash with the butter and milk, then season with salt and pepper.

To assemble the dish add the lentil mixture to a greased pie dish, tin, or similar (1.5L - 2L). Top with the mash and scatter over the grated cheddar.

Heat the oven to 190C/Fan 170C/Gas 5, then bake for 20-25 mins until the topping is golden.

Top Tip

You can vary the dish by changing the herbs to Indian spices and making a sweet potato or swede topping.

Main Meals

Shepherdess Pie

Prawn Curry

I love a prawn curry. There are so many variations and some of them are quite complex. This is my version, created after much experimenting. Tasty, quick and simple. Although the ingredients list is longish, once you've assembled the spices it's very quick. Serve with rice or Indian breads.

Ingredients

300g prawns drained. I use sustainable North Atlantic prawns or local langoustines. Use what you can get. Raw king prawns would work.
2 tbsp coconut oil
2 garlic cloves, crushed
'Thumb' of fresh root ginger, grated
1 small onion, finely chopped

1 small green chilli, de-seeded and finely chopped
2 tsp ground coriander
½ tsp turmeric
1 tsp salt
1 tbsp vinegar
1 tin of tomatoes
Leaf coriander to garnish

Method

Fry onion until soft and starting to brown, add the ginger, garlic and chilli and fry for a further 5 minutes until the garlic is cooked but not browning.

Add salt, turmeric and coriander and fry for a further minute.

Add the vinegar. Once the vinegar fumes have dissipated, add the tinned tomatoes and cook to reduce the sauce to a thick consistency. This takes around 25 minutes.

Add the drained prawns and heat through until hot - or cooked if raw - but don't allow to boil.

Serve with Indian breads and garnished with coriander.

Prawn Curry

HHC Chicken Curry

This is a fuss-free curry recipe. You can increase the chillis to turn up the heat, or omit them altogether if you want a mild fragrant curry. It will work well with pork if you prefer. The key to flavour is cooking the onions down and making sure the peppers are soft.

Ingredients

12 large chicken thighs, bone in
4 tbsp vegetable oil or sunflower oil
2 tsp cumin seeds
2 medium onions, sliced
3cm piece of fresh root ginger, peeled and shredded
3 fat garlic cloves, shredded
3 plump green chillies, halved lengthways (leave in some or all of the seeds if you like a hot curry)
½ tsp turmeric

½ tsp garam masala
2 tsp paprika
2 large peppers, one red and one yellow or orange, seeded and cut into rough chunks
2 tbsp tomato purée
coconut milk
3 tbsp chopped coriander, to serve
6 "cubes" of frozen spinach or a packet of fresh spinach, washed and chopped.

Method

Pull the skin off the chicken using kitchen paper to get a good grip. Set the chicken aside. Heat the oil in a large pan over a medium heat – a wok or deep saute pan works well for this.

Fry the cumin seeds for a few secs until they give off their aroma, then tip in the onions and turn the heat down low. Cook with the lid on until the onions are soft and squidgy, but not browning - about 10 mins.

Sprinkle in the ginger, garlic and chillies and fry for a minute or so, then sprinkle in the turmeric, garam masala and paprika. Stir in the chicken and peppers and continue frying for about 10 mins until the spice mixture clings to the chicken and the onions turn golden brown. Add a splash of water if they start to catch on the bottom of the pan.

Stir the tomato purée into the coconut milk, turn down the heat a fraction and stir the coconut milk into the pan followed by about 125ml cold water. At this point, scrape any sticky residue from the bottom of the pan and stir in.

Bring to a simmer and cook gently without a lid for about 30-35 mins until the chicken is tender and visibly coming away from the bone. Stir in a little more water if the sauce becomes dry – it should thicken and take on a warm reddish tinge. Season to taste. Garnish with the coriander leaf.

Serve with rice.

Top Tip

If you want to, you can bone the chicken at the end and put it back in the sauce. It's easier than trying to bone it raw if you're not an expert!

Chicken Curry

Snacks, Sides & Sauces

I wanted to include a section on snacks because, let's face it, most of us do it. You may be delighted - or possibly horrified - to find a section on snacking in a cookbook. There are a lot of myths surrounding snacking, including the one that all snacks are bad for you. Not all snacks are created equal and there are plenty of nutritious and satisfying snacks you can make easily. Forget what your mother told you; a snack will not ruin your meal (unless you have it 5 minutes before your meal that is...) It is actually more likely that you will eat less food if have a mid-morning or mid afternoon snack. I'm not talking about grazing all day on biscuits, crisps or chocolate, rather, munching on a considered range of little bites that you can rustle up, or pre-prepare, if the hours between meals seem to stretch out interminably.

So, dismiss the myths and embrace a few healthy HHC snacks.

I've also included a few sides and sauces in this section that you can eat with some of the other recipes in the book, with your own selections, or in some cases, stand-alone.

Easy Peasy Hummus

Hummus, or houmous, has become ubiquitous and can be found in supermarkets across the land. A good reason to make your own is that it's cheap and easy and won't contain any emulsifiers or hydrogenated fats. This recipe uses olive oil, but is lower fat than many recipes as it also uses some of the chickpea water to make the required consistency.

Ingredients

1 x 400g tin of chickpeas in water (no added salt or sugar)
1 small clove of garlic, minced
1 tbsp tahini
1 lemon, squeezed
extra virgin olive oil

Method

Drain the chickpeas, reserving a little of the liquid.

Add the chickpeas to the bowl of a food processor and then add the other ingredients, including a good squeeze of lemon juice and about a tablespoon of oil. Add a pinch of seal salt.

Blitz until smooth. If it seems a little dry, add some of the water you saved and/or a touch of oil. Use a spatula to scrape down the sides of the processor bowl and blitz again until you have a smooth mixture.

Taste and adjust the seasoning. If the mixture is still too stiff loosen it with lemon juice or a little more of the chickpea water until you have a consistency you're happy with.

Serve with batons of raw vegetables e.g. carrots, onions, broccoli, cauli, mushrooms, etc. or the oatcakes on page 116.

Top Tip

For an alternative hummus, use 200g cooked beetroot (not pickled), half tin (200g) of chickpeas, 50g ground nuts, oil and lemon, to make a colourful and interesting version.

GF

Easy Peasy Hummus

Paupers Pesto

If you grow your own basil, getting your hands on large bunches is easy, but if you're relying on local stores, try Asian grocers where you can often find large bunches of basil and coriander fairly cheaply. You can also buy supermarket growing pots, but make sure you pot the plants up into a couple of new pots or they will reliably die on you.

The classic Italian pesto is made with basil, olive oil, Parmesan and pine nuts. Pine nuts have become increasingly expensive over the years and more difficult to get hold of, so I developed this alternative using sunflower and pumpkin seeds instead. It's not the classic recipe, but it's just as good, and a whole lot cheaper to make.

Ingredients

1 clove garlic
1 big bunch of fresh basil
50g sunflower seeds and pumpkin seeds
50g freshly grated Parmesan cheese
150ml extra virgin olive oil
Juice of 1 lemon (optional)

Method

Blitz the seeds in a mini processor, spice grinder or similar. Add the basil and olive oil and whiz to a smooth paste. Remove to a bowl and stir in the finely grated cheese and check for taste. I like to add a touch of lemon juice to keep the colour and avoid adding extra salt. Adjust to your own taste. Beat in the lemon juice, if using. This will keep in an airtight container in the fridge for around a week - if it lasts that long!

Serve simply with pasta, or add to soups, or even sandwiches instead of mayonnaise.

Bliss Balls

I devised these power-packed morsels in 2016 when my husband was looking for protein snacks after swim and weight training sessions. I didn't realise then that they were a 'thing'. Trendy or not, they're tasty and transportable, and you can vary the ingredients infinitely, including using savoury elements. You will need a food processor or mini chopper to make these. You can make them by hand if you don't have a processor, but use ground nuts and seeds and chop the dried fruit thoroughly. Mix in a large bowl.

I offer here, three of my favourite protein snack balls. You can use the basic recipe to invent your own. They're very versatile.

These recipes make 16 -20 balls depending on how big you make them.

Ingredients (Black Forest Bliss Balls)

125g almonds
125g dried sour cherries (or glace if preferred)
125g dried dates (pitted)
2 tbsp raw cacao powder or unsweetened cocoa powder & extra to coat

1 tbsp nut butter (your choice)
¼ tsp nutmeg
11/2 tbsp cherry juice or orange juice

Ingredients (Gingerbread)

125g raisins
125g dates
125g walnuts

1 tbsp black strap molasses or black treacle
1 tsp ground ginger

Ingredients (Peanut Butter & Coconut)

140g crunchy peanut butter - use peanut butter without palm oil
140g dates
20g coconut oil

30g ground seeds (flax, hemp, sesame, your choice)
20g ground almonds
20g oats
20g Dessicated coconut and extra to coat

Method

Put all the ingredients in the bowl of a food processor and pulse until the mixture is finely chopped and blended (30 - 50 seconds).

Wet your hands so they're damp and shape the mixture into even size balls. Dust in:

- cocoa or cacao powder (for Black Forest Bliss Balls)
- oats, if a bit sticky, or leave plain (for Gingerbread Bliss Balls)
- dessicated coconut (for Peanut Butter & Coconut Bliss Balls)

Chill on trays in the fridge for 30 minutes before storing in the fridge in an airtight container.

Tamari Baked Seeds

These make a surprisingly tasty snack that you can feel quite virtuous about. Don't leave the seeds in the oven too long or you'll burn them. Cooking at low temperature preserves the oils better. They keep for a few weeks in an airtight tub.

Ingredients

50g sunflower seeds, raw
50g pumpkin seeds, raw
1 tbsp tamari (or soy sauce*)

Method

Preheat the oven to 150C/130C Fan/Gas 2.

Pour all the seeds into a mixing bowl, drizzle over the tamari (or soy sauce*) and mix well with a spoon.

Spread the seeds thinly on a baking tray and bake.

Roast for 10-15 minutes or until golden brown, checking every 5 minutes or so, and giving the tray a shake so they don't stick or burn.

* Won't be GF if you use Soy Sauce; Tamari is GF.

Eggs-in-a-Mug

This is a 'tweak' on something my dad used to eat as a mid-week supper. It's simple, nutritious, and for time-limited cooks, FAST! Add some bread and you have something a bit more filling.

Ingredients

2 hard-boiled eggs (about 7- 8 minutes)
1 large cornichon (pickled or brined gherkin), finely chopped
2 scallions or a shallot, finely chopped
2 tsp. capers, chopped if large
A knob of butter, dash of cold pressed oil or spoonful of mayonnaise

Method

Boil the eggs until hard. Cool in cold water. Peel the eggs, place in a bowl and lightly chop. Add the fat, if using, and the other ingredients. Place in a large mug and eat with a teaspoon!

This can be served hot if you prefer. It also makes a good sandwich filling - a change from egg mayonnaise.

Tamari Baked Seeds (top) - Eggs-in-a-Mug (bottom)

Artichoke & White Bean Pâté

I sometimes whiz this up as a lunch, served with raw veg and the oatcakes on p116. More often it sits as a dip in the fridge, ready to be pressed into service when tummies rumble. It won't freeze, but it keeps well refrigerated in an airtight container.

Ingredients

1 tin artichokes
½ tin cannellini beans (haricot or butter beans can be used instead)
juice of half a lemon
½ clove garlic
olive oil

Method

Place the artichokes, beans and garlic in a food processor, or use a hand held blitzer to blend to a smooth puree. Add the oil a little at a time to make a consistency you like. Add lemon juice to taste. Serve at room temperature. Refrigerate to store.

Cheesy Olives

These are a bit fussy to knock-up mid-week if you're busy, but they're not difficult. Make them at the weekend for ultra-savoury nibbles during the week - If you can leave them that long! They'll keep in an airtight container for a week and can be popped back in the oven to warm if they happen to last long enough to go soggy.

Ingredients

200g self raising flour
100g butter, softened
150g mature cheddar cheese grated
(at room temperature)
pinch of caynenne pepper

pinch of paprika
few twists of black pepper
½ teaspoon ground dried mustard
25 to 30 olives of your choice, stoned

Method

Preheat the oven to 200C/180C Fan/Gas 6 and grease a baking tray.

In a bowl, combine the flour, butter and cheese and seasonings (optional). Make into a small balls with your hands (roughly meatball sized) then slip an olive into the centre of the ball and close the dough around it so it is covered, pressing it together.

Arrange on the prepared baking tray and bake in the preheated oven for 15-20 minutes until golden brown.

Remove from the oven and allow to cool completely on the tray. They will be very soft at this stage so are difficult to handle. Pack in an airtight container.

Try not to eat the whole lot in one go (yes, we've done it!)

Artichoke & White Bean Pâté

Spicy Chickpeas

This works better with dried, cooked chickpeas, rather than tinned. But if tinned is all you have, make sure you drain them thoroughly and dry them on kitchen paper. Serves 2-4 for nibbles.

Ingredients

200g of dried chickpeas cooked or
400g can of chickpeas drained and dried
½ tsp chilli
1 tsp za'atar
pinch of sea salt
1 tbsp olive oil

Method

Place the oil and spices in a roomy bowl. Tip in the chickpeas and mix around until they are well coated.

Heat the oven 200C/180C Fan/Gas 6.

Place the coated chickpeas onto a lined baking tray and roast for 25 minutes until the chickpeas are crispy.

Allow to cool before sprinkling with the salt.

Store in an airtight container.

Oatcakes

There are probably as many recipes for oatcakes as there are people in the Highlands. This is based on a traditional Orkney recipe, with a Highland Home Cook tweak.

Ingredients

40g medium oatmeal
140g porridge oats
tsp freshly ground black pepper
½ tsp salt
75ml extra-virgin olive oil
boiling water

Method

Preheat the oven to 180C/160C Fan/Gas 4 and dust two baking trays with flour.

Mix all the dry ingredients in a bowl. Pour the oil into a well in the centre, then pour in enough boiling water to bind it into a firm, but not too sticky, dough. If you add too much water, don't worry you can rectify it with a bit of extra oatmeal.

Squish the dough mixture together with your hands to form a ball (it should hold together and leave the bowl clean). Leave it to rest for a few minutes. Roll out the dough on a floured surface to about 5mm thick. Don't be afraid to use more flour if it's a bit sticky.

Top Tip

Use your hands to squish the mix together. The oats and oil will make your skin lovely and soft!

Cut out discs with a biscuit cutter - I use a small one (about 5cm) but it's up to you.

Use a palette knife or a fish slice to transfer them onto the baking trays. Bake them for around 20 minutes, then turn them over and bake for a further 5-10 minutes. Keep an eye that they don't go too brown.

Cool on a rack, then store in an airtight container. They'll keep for a week or more if you've baked them well and allowed them to cool properly.

I'm happy to eat them 'naked', as a snack, but you can add your favourite topping to make them more substantial or serve them with the pate or hummus in this chapter.

Spicy Vegetables & Potato Wedges

This is a versatile duo of sides which will go with any number of mains. Served together they even make a main meal of their own. The veg can be used with the wraps and polenta recipes on page 95 as an alternative to the one given or eaten next day, with a salad dressing.

Ingredients

For the vegetables:
1 small-medium butternut squash (around 1kg)
1 red onion, halved and thickly sliced
3 mixed peppers cut into 1cm wide strips
2 garlic cloves, finely chopped
4 tbsp olive oil
3 tbsp curry powder
large handful coriander, chopped

For the Wedges:
800g potatoes, such as Desiree, washed
3 tbsp olive oil
3 garlic cloves, finely chopped
½ tsp paprika
1 tsp medium chilli powder
1 tsp onion powder
1 tsp celery seed
1 tsp dried mixed herbs

Method

Heat oven to 200C/180C Fan/Gas 6.

For the vegetables:
Using a peeler, peel the butternut squash. Cut it in half lengthways, scoop out the seeds, then cut into 1cm-thick cubes.

Put the squash cubes in a large roasting tin with the onion, peppers and garlic. Mix the oil with the curry powder and drizzle over the vegetables. Toss well to coat in the curry mix and season.

Roast for 30 mins until the vegetables are beginning to soften.

For the wedges:
Cut the potatoes into wedge shapes. Combine the ingredients with the oil and seasoning. Toss the potatoes around in the mixture. Lay the potatoes on a baking tray in a single layer and roast for 30 minutes, along with the vegetables above.

Serve either dish as a "side" or together if you want to make a larger meal.

Seedy Spiced Roast Potatoes

This is a speedier, healthier version of the classic Indian accompaniment. It goes with all sorts of dishes, not just Indian ones.

Serves 4.

Ingredients

350g potatoes, boiled and cut into 2cm cubes
¼ tsp mustard seeds
¼ tsp cumin
¼ tsp fennel
¼ tsp nigella
¼ tsp fenugreek
½ tsp turmeric powder

1 tbsp tomato puree
2 pinches of chilli powder
3 tbsps olive oil
6 cherry tomatoes halved
½ bunch of spring onions, finely sliced
leaf coriander to garnish, chopped
salt and pepoer to taste

Method

Put the oil in a bowl and add the seeds, turmeric, chilli powder, tomato puree and salt.

Add the potatoes and mix until evenly coated. I use my hands.

Place on a lined baking tray and cook 200C/180C Fan/Gas 6.for 20 minutes. After 20 minutes, sprinkle over the halved cherry tomatoes and spring onions. Add an extra lick of olive oil if it looks a bit dry. Cook for a further 10 minutes. Garnish with the coriander to serve.

GF

Cheaty Cheese Sauce

If you want a rich sauce and don't have a lot of time, or worry about making a roux, this cheaty version is ideal. Simple and very quick. Use it for a quick pasta dish or in a lasagne.

Ingredients

100g grated mature cheddar
250g mascarpone
100ml whole milk
1 tbsp mustard to taste.

Method

Place the mascarpone in a pan and heat gently. Add the cheddar and allow to melt slowly. Whatever you do, don't boil it. Add enough milk to make the sauce a consistency that you like. Add the mustard if liked. Adjust seasoning to taste.

Kiwi Salsa

This makes a nice salsa to serve with fish dishes, but you can serve it with anything you fancy.

Ingredients

3 just-ripe kiwi, peeled and diced
½ bunch spring onions, finely sliced
Juice of 1 lime
½ a chilli - or according to your own taste
Coriander and basil leaf, chopped, to serve

Method

Add the ingredients, except the herbs, to a bowl and mix together.

Leave for 15 minutes for the flavours to amalgamate.

Garnish with the herbs.

Top Tip

If you have any left over, you can blitz it and use it as a sauce.

Kiwi Salsa

Proper Puddings

I'm not a massive pudding lover as I don't have much of a sweet tooth. I do enjoy making puddings for others to enjoy, and will happily indulge in a 'proper' pudding occasionally.

In a lot of my recipes I try to reduce the sugar content. Even if you have a sweet tooth, do give them a try as they are first and see how you get on, I hope you will be pleasantly surprised.

Cranberry & Orange Cheesecake

This is an easy, yet impressive cheesecake. It isn't particularly sweet, so if you have a sweet tooth, add extra sugar to the topping.

Ingredients

Base:
1 pkt ginger biscuits (180g-200g) crushed
75g butter, melted

Cranberry Topping:
150g cranberries (fresh or frozen)
50g sugar, to your taste
1 orange, zest and juice
½ tsp ground ginger
½ tsp cinnamon

Filling:
125g crowdie (or 250g mascarpone if you can't get hold of crowdie)
125g mascarpone
150ml plain yoghurt
200ml double cream
zest of whole orange
juice of ½ orange
50-75g caster sugar

Method

First, make the base. Melt the butter and add the crushed biscuits. Spread across a lined spring-form or loose-bottomed cake tin (20cm). Allow to cool.

Meanwhile, cook the cranberries with the orange juice, zest, sugar and spices. Allow to break down and thicken. There is no thickening agent in this recipe, so make sure you cook the cranberries down properly. They'll thicken a little more when cooled. Allow to cool thoroughly.

For the body of the cheesecake, put the cream cheese(s) and sugar into a large bowl and mix to blend. Add the cream and yoghurt and beat to mix. You can use electric hand held whisk or food processor for this stage, if you wish. Now gradually add the lemon juice, little by little, until it's all incorporated. Spread this mixture over the base and chill until firm, or for at least 4 hours.

Spread the cooled cranberry mixture over the top and serve.

Puddings

Cranberry & Orange Cheesecake

Rhubarb & Strawberry Oaty Crumble

Who doesn't love a crumble? This version pairs early season rhubarb with the first of the summer strawberries and an interesting crunchy topping. Use the recipe with any fruit of your choice, if you're not a fan of rhubarb.

Ingredients

For the filling:
650g rhubarb
250g strawberries
80g golden caster sugar
2 basil leaves, finely chopped
2 mint leaves, finely chopped

For the crumble:
80g oats
30g mixed seeds: e.g. sunflower and pumpkin
75g chilled butter, cut into small pieces
175g self-raising flour
1 tsp mixed spice (sweet)
1 tsp ground ginger
100g demerara sugar

Method

Cut any leaves off the rhubarb and wash. Cut into 2.5cm pieces then toss them in a bowl with the sugar and strawberries. Next, place them in a baking dish and keep to one side.

To make the crumble in a food processor all you do is place the butter, sifted flour, spices and sugar in the processor and pulse until it resembles fine breadcrumbs. Remove to a bowl and mix in the oats and seeds.

If you don't have a food processor, rub the butter into the flour and sugar in a large bowl until it resembles breadcrumb texture, then proceed as above.

Next, sprinkle the crumble mixture all over the rhubarb and strawberry mixture, spreading it right up to the edges of the dish, lightly pressing it down with your hand. Now, bake the crumble on the centre shelf of the oven for 35-40 minutes, 200C/180C Fan/Gas 6. Allow to rest for 10 minutes before serving with cream, ice cream or custard.

Puddings

HHC Classic Sticky Toffee Pudding

There is some debate about whether the original pudding does indeed hale from Cartmel in the Lake District, in the 70's, or whether it originated from Scotland, and much further back. Debate aside, this is a light date sponge with a rich sticky sauce. It's worth making the quantity in the recipe. I defy you to have any left, and if you do, it freezes like a dream.

Ingredients

For the pudding:
225g whole Medjool dates, pitted
175g boiling water
1 tsp vanilla extract
175g self-raising flour, plus extra for greasing
1 tsp bicarbonate of soda
2 eggs
85g butter, softened, plus extra for greasing
140g demerara sugar
2 tbsp black strap molasses or black treacle
100ml milk

For the toffee sauce:
175g light muscovado sugar
50g butter, cut into pieces
225ml double cream
1 tbsp black strap molasses or black treacle

Method

Chop the dates quite small, or chop in a food processor. Put them in a bowl, then pour the boiling water over. Leave for about 30 mins until cool and well-soaked, then mash a bit with a fork. Stir in the vanilla extract.

Grease a square or rectangular cake tin and sit on a baking sheet. Heat oven to 180C/160C Fan/Gas 4.

While the dates are soaking, make the puddings. Mix the flour and bicarbonate of soda together. Beat the eggs in a separate bowl. Beat the butter and sugar together in a large bowl for a few mins until light and creamy. The mixture will still be grainy, but don't worry.

Add the eggs a little at a time, beating well between additions. Beat in the molasses or treacle, then, using a large metal spoon, gently fold in one-third of the flour, then half the milk. Don't over beat. Repeat until all the flour and milk is used.

Stir the soaked dates into the pudding batter. The mix may look a little curdled and will be a soft thick batter rather than a firm cake mix. Spoon it into the tin and bake for 20-25 mins, until risen and firm.

To make the sauce, put the sugar and butter in a medium saucepan with half the cream. Bring to the boil over a medium heat, stirring all the time, until the sugar has completely dissolved. Stir in the molasses or treacle, then turn up the heat slightly and let the mixture bubble away for 2-3 mins. until it's a rich toffee colour, stirring occasionally to make sure it doesn't burn.

Take the pan off the heat and beat in the rest of the cream. Serve with squares of the pudding.

> **Top Tip**
>
> Use a hot spoon to make measuring the treacle/molasses easier.

Puddings

HHC Classic Sticky Toffee Pudding

Chocolate Whisky Truffle Tart

This is essentially a chocolate whisky truffle mix made into a dessert, with the addition of a biscuit topping and a little syrup in the mixture to make the texture a little softer and add a little sweetness. It is a very rich dessert and small portions are advised. Great with coffee for a sweet treat.

Ingredients

400g dark chocolate (minimum 70% cocoa solids)
5 tbsp golden syrup
5 tbsp Scottish whisky
570ml double cream, ambient temperature
75g Bourbon biscuits, crushed very finely (a food processor is easiest but you can use a rolling pin)

Method

Begin by sprinkling the crushed Bourbon creams all over the base of a lined and greased, 23cm loose-bottomed cake tin or spring-form tin.

Next, break the chocolate up into pieces and put them in a heat-proof bowl together with the golden syrup. Sit the bowl over a saucepan of barely simmering water. It's important that the bowl of chocolate does not make contact with the water and that the water doesn't boil, as this could make the chocolate seize. Do not use a microwave! Stir occasionally until melted and combined. Remove from the heat and leave the mixture to cool for 5 minutes or so. Add the whisky.

Now, in a separate bowl, beat the cream to the soft stage stage. It should not be stiff and holding peaks, but just thickened. Fold half the cream into the chocolate mixture and then fold that mixture into the rest of the cream. When it is smoothly blended, spoon it into the prepared tin. Cover and chill overnight.

Just before serving, run a flat knife round the edge to loosen the tart, then give it a good shake and turn the whole thing out on to a serving plate. It should be inverted so the bottom of dish, which has the crushed biscuits, is now on the top.

Don't worry, it's well behaved!

This is a very rich tart and will serve 8 - 10 people easily.

Suitable for freezing, but portion it first.

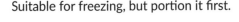

Chocolate Whisky Truffle Tart

Rich Lemon Cream

This is a case of combining a few ingredients and chilling. I adapted a friend's lemon flan recipe from a million years ago and this was the result. It's sweet, smooth and rich, so serve it with a biscuit of some sort (the shortbread in the baking section on p142 would be ideal).

Ingredients

150ml double cream - I use organic as I find it has more flavour
1 tin of condensed milk
2 large (organic) unwaxed lemons, juice from both and zest from one

Method

Tip the condensed milk into a roomy bowl and add the double cream. Add the zested peel from the lemons and trickle in the lemon juice a bit at a time, whilst beating the mixture. It will thicken.

Check for taste after each addition of lemon juice. You may not need all the juice. It depends on how large the lemons are and how lemony you like things.

Tip into a serving dish - I use a soufflé dish - and chill for at least 4 hours.

Dollop spoonfuls into glass dishes and enjoy!

Top Tip

Serve the lemon cream in a pre-made flan case if you want an easy dessert to serve to friends.

Puddings

Rich Lemon Cream

Blackberry Pudding

With thanks to Lynn Cole who first cooked this for me, and then gave me a copy of the recipe. This is adapted from the original.

Ingredients

200g blackberries
60g caster sugar
1 tbsp ginger wine or orange juice
100g self-raising flour

50g butter
150ml semi-skimmed milk
icing sugar to dust (optional)

Method

Preheat oven to 200C/180C Fan/Gas 6.

Sprinkle blackberries with 1 tablespoon of caster sugar and the ginger wine or juice. Set aside.

Sift the flour into a large bowl and rub in the butter until it looks like fine breadcrumbs. Stir in remaining sugar and then pour in the milk to make batter. Note: this will be lumpy

Place the blackberries into a (1L) oven-proof dish, reserving some of the juices to serve with the cooked pudding.

Pour the batter over the blackberries. Place the dish on a baking tray and bake for 30-40 minutes until risen and golden brown

Allow to cool slightly before serving, dusted with icing sugar, if you wish, and served with the reserved juice.

Lemon Delicious Pudding

Lemon Delicious Pudding is also variously known as self-saucing pudding, Lemon Surprise Pudding and Magic Lemon Pudding.

This is another easy and reliable dessert, which reputedly has been around for centuries. Making sure the butter, milk and eggs are at room temperature will help them blend, but don't worry if you left them in the fridge. Ignore the oddly curdled batter. It will bake into a light dreamy sponge with lemon sauce.

Serves 4 (or two greedy people!)

Ingredients
50g butter
200g golden caster sugar
2-3 (organic) unwaxed lemons to make 100ml juice plus grated zest of 1 lemon
3 eggs, separated,
50g plain flour, sifted
250ml milk

Method
First, heat the oven to 180C/160C Fan/Gas 4.

Beat the butter, sugar and lemon zest until they are pale and creamy. I use an electric hand whisk but you can use a food processor. Add the lemon juice, yolks, flour and milk one by one until you have a smooth batter. Whisk the egg whites until firm but not stiff, and fold these into the batter.

Pour into a buttered, oven-proof soufflé dish (1L) or baking dish. Bake for 35-45 minutes until the top is lightly browned and set. There should be a lemon curd type sauce underneath.

Puddings

Crowdie & Jam no-churn Ice Cream

When I first started my food business, my freezers were so packed that I didn't have room to freeze the bowl from my ice-cream maker. As a result I came up with several recipes for 'no-churn' ice cream that turn out a smooth and delicious ice-cream with little fuss.

Ingredients

300ml tub of (organic) double cream
160g tub of crowdie or mascarpone
1 jar of jam (min 370g) fruit of your choice. Blackcurrant and raspberry work well
2 tbsp plain live yoghurt

Method

Place the cream cheese in a bowl and beat to loosen. Beat in the double cream and yoghurt. You can do this with an electric hand whisk if you like. When the ingredients are combined to a smooth mixture (crowdie is naturally a little grainy so don't worry about this) fold in the jam. Freeze in a plastic container for 6 - 8 hours (overnight), or until frozen.

Puddings

Traditional Christmas Pudding

I know. It's probably not Christmas when you're reading this and you're wondering why I've included a Christmas recipe in a general cookbook. The reason is simple. I've been asked for the recipe so many times, I thought I'd put it here for posterity. If you like Christmas pudding, you'll like this. It's slightly lighter in colour and spicing than the dark pudding you may be used to, but none the worse for that.

Ingredients

200g raisins
200g sultanas
120g self-raising flour
200g finely grated butter (freeze it before you grate it, and dust it with flour)
60g fresh brown breadcrumbs (from around 4 thick slices of bread)
180g light muscovado sugar

½ carrot, grated
1 tsp ground cinnamon
1 tsp ground mixed spice
½ tsp ground ginger
250ml stout (or milk, if you prefer)
1 large egg
butter, for greasing

Method

Put all the ingredients into a large bowl and make sure they are mixed. Divide into 1 large, 2 small or 4 mini pudding basins.

Cover with a circle of greaseproof and a double layer of foil, making a pleat in the centre to allow the pudding to rise. Tie the foil securely with string, then place in a steamer or large pan containing enough gently simmering water to come halfway up the sides of the bowl.

Steam, covered with a lid, for 2½ hours. Or follow the instructions for your pressure cooker, if you have one (a pre-steam without pressure is necessary for this recipe to rise). Check the water level during cooking, topping up if necessary.

If you are preparing this pudding ahead, remove the foil, let the pudding cool slightly, then wrap in greaseproof paper and fresh foil. Don't let the foil touch the pudding or the foil will corrode.

Baking

From fancy cakes to tea loaves and biscuits, everyone likes a bit of baking, so delve in and enjoy. What follows in this section are some of the most popular bakes I have made for the community markets.

Double Chocolate Brownies

There are many recipes for brownies. I hope this will become one of your favourites. It's always very popular at Highland markets.

There's a lot of chocolate in these, but don't skimp! If you don't fancy bashing chocolate up – I confess I quite enjoy it - you can use chocolate chips, but it won't be quite the same. Part of the joy of these brownies is discovering varying size chunks of chocolate, if you serve them cold, or molten puddles of chocolate, if you serve them warm.

Makes 24 small squares.

Ingredients

300g plain chocolate broken into pieces
225g butter
1 tsp vanilla extract
2 tbsp hot water
3 large eggs
225g caster sugar
75g self-raising flour

Method

Grease and line a 30x23cm brownie tin or roasting tin with greaseproof paper or baking parchment.

Put 250g ONLY* of the chocolate and butter in a bowl and sit over a small pan of gently simmering water. Melt the chocolate slowly, then remove the bowl from the pan and let the chocolate cool down. Don't boil this or let the water touch the bowl or the chocolate may sieze.

In another bowl, beat the eggs and sugar. Use an electric hand whisk. Next, add the cooled – not cold - chocolate mixture. Add a tablespoon of hot water to the mix and beat in, along with the vanilla extract.

Fold in the flour then the remaining 50g of chocolate, broken up into smallish 'chips'.

Pour the mixture into the prepared tin and bake in a preheated oven at 190C/170C Fan/Gas 5 for about 30-35 minutes or until firm to the touch. The top will look dull and crisp and has characteristic cracks. Don't be tempted to overcook or the middle will not be nice and gooey.

Leave to cool in the tin, then cut into 24 pieces.

*if you prefer a traditional brownie without the extra chocolate pieces, put all 300g of chocolate into the bowl to melt. It won't be a 'double-chocolate' brownie, but it will be every bit as chocolatey and delicious!

HHC Double Chocolate Brownies

The Best Ginger Shortbread

Crisp, crunchy and melt-in-the-mouth, who doesn't like shortbread? As a ginger fiend, this spiced up version can't be beaten. If you're a purist, leave it out. This recipe will guarantee you lovely crumbly buttery-ness every time. Use the best ingredients you can afford. There are so few, it makes a difference!

This makes quite a small quantity, but it saves us gorging ourselves on shortbread!

Makes around 12.

Ingredients

115g lightly salted organic butter, must be at room temperature
55g golden caster sugar
130g plain flour
30g ground rice
10g cornflour
2 tsp ground ginger

Method

Line a rectangular baking tray.

Pre-heat the oven to 160C/140 Fan/Gas 3.

Put the butter into a large mixing bowl, and beat with a wooden spoon until soft. Then beat in the sugar. You should have a light, creamy mixture.

Add the flour, cornflour, ground-rice and ginger and work quickly to form a smooth dough; if it doesn't come together, add a touch more butter.

Lightly pat out the dough to ½cm thickness and cut into rectangular biscuit shapes. You can roll out and put the mixture into a cake tin if you like, but do it quickly and don't press too hard. Use a fork or docker to imprint 'holes' in the dough. Put in the fridge to chill for 15 minutes, until firm.

Top Tip

They're called "short bread" for a reason. Don't be tempted to move them from the tray too soon or you'll end up with crumbs!

Bake for around 25-35 minutes, until cooked through, but not browned. This will very much depend on your oven and how thick you have rolled out the dough.

Allow to cool for a couple of minutes (to solidify) then transfer to a wire rack.

Once cold, this should last for a good few days in an airtight container, but we usually manage to eat them a lot quicker!

Baking

Ginger Shortbread

Courgette & Lime Cake

This is a moist cake, which keeps well. It's not too sweet and has the advantage of using up a courgette glut in the summer.

I use plain brown flour, but use white if you prefer.

Makes 8 generous slices.

Ingredients
2 large eggs
125ml vegetable oil
85g soft brown sugar
350g courgette, coarsely grated, liquid squeezed out using a tea-towel
Grated rind of 2 limes
300g plain brown flour
½ tsp bicarbonate of soda
½ tsp baking powder

Method
Heat the oven to 180C/160C Fan/Gas 4. Grease and line a 2lb loaf tin with baking parchment.

In a large bowl, whisk the eggs, oil and sugar, then add the courgettes and lime rind.

In a separate bowl, combine the dry ingredients with a pinch of salt. Stir these into the wet mixture, then pour into the tin.

Bake for about an hour, or until a skewer inserted into the centre of the cake comes out clean.

Allow to cool. Serve decorated with lime zest, lime curd or a thin lemon and lime icing. If you're going to freeze this cake, do so before adding any topping.

Top Tip

Make sure you get the liquid out of the courgettes or your cake will be soggy.

Baking

Seasonal Fruit Drizzle Cake

This is drizzle cake cranked up a notch. You can make it with summer berries - fresh or frozen - autumn stone fruit, or even dried fruit (soaked) if you have nothing else. I've successfully made blueberry, blackberry, blackcurrant and rhubarb versions.

Makes 8 generous slices.

Ingredients

2 large, organic, free-range eggs
100g fruit, weight stoned, cored, seeded, etc.
2 tbsp citrus juice - lemon, lime or orange
175g soft butter (plus extra for greasing)
175g golden caster sugar

250g self-raising flour

For the topping:
75g fruit, weight stoned, cored, seeded, etc.
140g granulated sugar
1-2 tbsp citrus juice

Method

Put 75g of fruit in a bowl and leave to one side.

Heat the oven to 180C/160C Fan/Gas 4. Grease a 900g/2lb loaf tin and line the base and ends with a long strip of baking parchment.

Put the butter, caster sugar, flour and eggs into a large bowl and beat with an electric hand mixer for around 5 mins until pale and fluffy. It will be quite thick. Add a couple of spoons of the citrus juice of your choice and stir in.

Spread one-third of the cake mix into your tin, then spread over 50g of the fruit, being careful not to press it into the cake mixture. Next, "dot" and spread another third of the cake mix on top, then scatter with another 50g fruit. Finally, "dot" the rest of the cake mix over the top and gently spread with the back of a wet spoon.

Bake for about an hour, or until an inserted skewer comes out clean.

Meanwhile stir a tablespoon or two of the citrus juice into the fruit you've set aside and add the granulated sugar. Mash a little of the fruit with a fork. If it seems too dry, add some more citrus juice. The consistency will depend on the fruit you're using.

Leave the cake in the tin and poke the cake all over with a skewer then spoon the fruit and sugar mix over the cake. Leave in the tin until the cake is cool and the topping is set and crisp.

Top Tip

For this one-step cake, it's important that the ingredients are at room temperature and the butter very soft, or it won't blend properly.

Baking

Seasonal Fruit Drizzle Cake

Bara Brith, or Scottish Tea Loaf

Translating as 'mottled bread', there are numerous recipes for this fruit tea loaf, including Irish and Welsh versions. This Scottish version was given to my by my 'Aunty' Gladys - A.K.A Topsy Wilson - who, interestingly, was from Yorkshire, not Scotland. Whatever her origins, she was a baking supremo and is sorely missed - and not just for her baking.

Ingredients

125g sultanas
125g raisins
150g soft dark brown sugar
225g self-raising flour
1 large, organic, free-range egg, beaten
300ml strong hot tea, I use Assam or afternoon tea, but any brew will work
1tbsp Seville orange marmalade
1tbsp black treacle or blackstrap molasses
2 tsp mixed spice (optional)

Method

Begin the day before you bake the loaf cake by soaking the fruit and sugar in the hot tea overnight.

Next day, preheat the oven to 170C/150C Fan/Gas 3. Line a 900g/2lb loaf tin with baking parchment.

Add all the remaining ingredients to the fruit and tea mix and stir well. Empty into the prepared loaf tin.

Bake for about one hour. If the top is browning too much, cover with foil.

Cool on a wire rack. Serve thickly sliced, spread with butter.

Baking

Lemon Polenta Cake with Rosemary

I first ate this cake in the mid 80's at a family-run hotel in an Italian ski resort. The panettiere, who spoke very little English, kindly gave me the recipe. At the time, I'd never heard of polenta, but I've since devised many cakes using it.

It makes a great gluten-free bake, if you use gluten-free baking powder.

Ingredients

2 lemons, unwaxed, organic
140g butter, softened (plus extra for greasing)
3 eggs
250g golden caster sugar
200g ground almonds
175g polenta (or fine cornmeal)
1 tsp gluten-free baking powder

For the drizzle:
150 golden caster sugar
juice of 2 lemons (and water, if necessary, to make up to 150 ml)
1 sprig rosemary (plus some chopped, to decorate)

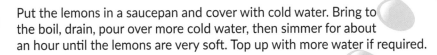

Method

Grease a 23cm cake tin and heat an oven to 180C/160C Fan/Gas 4.

Put the lemons in a saucepan and cover with cold water. Bring to the boil, drain, pour over more cold water, then simmer for about an hour until the lemons are very soft. Top up with more water if required.

Drain the lemons well. When cool, halve them and remove the pips. Blitz to a purée in a food processor.

Add all the other cake ingredients and carry on blitzing until you have a loose batter.

Scrape the batter into the cake tin and bake for 40-50 mins until golden and starting to shrink away from the sides.

While the cake bakes, make the rosemary drizzle. Mix the sugar with the lemon juice and water, if necessary. Add the rosemary sprig and heat in a small pan. Bubble the mixture until syrupy. About 10 minutes or so.

Allow to cool.

When the cake is ready, remove from the oven and leave to cool a little. Make some holes in the cake with a cake tester and whilst the cake is still warm, pour over the drizzle.

Sprinkle with some chopped rosemary, if you like. I've sometimes candied some rosemary to garnish the cake with.

Top Tip

This cake works equally well with oranges, but make sure you don't exceed the liquid quantity. Leave out the rosemary if you don't like it.

Baking

Lemon Polenta Cake

Strawberry and Polenta Cakes

These little cakes are the essence of summer. Great to bring out at a sharing picnic. I'm not a fan of icing, but this fresh strawberry version is delightful. Guaranteed to please young people and adults alike!

Ingredients

140g butter, softened
140g golden caster sugar
½ lemon grated zest
85g polenta
3 eggs, beaten
140g plain flour
1 tsp baking powder
1 tbsp milk

140g strawberries, hulled and chopped into pieces

To decorate:
150g icing sugar
6 strawberries, hulled and roughly chopped, plus 6 halved, for decoration
lemon juice

Method

Line a 12-hole muffin pan or bun tin with paper cases and heat the oven to 180C/160C Fan/Gas 4.

In a large bowl, cream together the butter, sugar and lemon zest until pale and fluffy. Add the polenta and continue to whisk until combined. Beat in the eggs, a little at a time.

Sift in the flour and baking powder, then fold in quickly with a large spoon. You should now have a thick batter. Don't worry if it looks a bit lumpy, the polenta means it won't be smooth. Stir in the milk to loosen, then gently fold in the chopped strawberries.

Top Tip

The cooled cakes will keep for a few days in an airtight container before icing them.

Divide the mixture between the paper cases, then bake for 15-20 mins or until golden brown, risen and springy to the touch. Place the cakes on a wire rack to cool completely.

Sift the icing sugar into a large bowl. Place the chopped strawberries in a bowl with 1 teaspoon of lemon juice and mash with a fork until pulpy. Push through a sieve over the icing sugar. You're aiming for a thick paste that is still fluid. Add more lemon, a drip at a time, if required.

Carefully remove the paper cases from the cakes, then dip the top of each cake into the icing, then top immediately with a strawberry half. Leave to set, then serve.

Baking

Lemon Yoghurt Cake

I tasted a version of this cake for breakfast, in Brittany, in the mid 80's, but could never find a recipe.

I've tried various recipes over the years, without much success; never finding anything approaching the original French cake. The recipe that follows is as close as I've come to it.

It won't win any awards for beauty but it tastes fantastic.

Ingredients
3 large, organic, free-range eggs
300g caster sugar
245g full-fat lemon curd yoghurt (you can use plain if you prefer, but it must be "full fat")
350g flour
50g ground almonds
2 lemons, zested, plus juice of ½ lemon (about 1 tbsp)
80g extra virgin olive oil
80g melted butter
2 tsp baking powder

Method

Preheat the oven to 160C/140C Fan/Gas 3.

Whisk the eggs with the sugar, lemon zest and juice with an electric hand beater, until pale in colour. Add the extra virgin olive oil, melted butter and yoghurt, and stir together.

Sift in the flour and the baking powder. Fold in until mixed well.

Grease and flour a 24cm round cake tin. Scrape the batter into the tin and bake for about 40-50 minutes until golden and dry inside.

The key to this cake is the cooking, so use a cake tester or toothpick to check it is completely dry. If it isn't, return to the oven for 5-10 more minutes and test again.

Once cooked, remove from the oven. Let it cool for 10 minutes then remove from the cake tin.

Allow to cool on wire cooling rack. Decorate with icing sugar and zested lemon peel, if you'd like to pretty it up. Serve with soft fruit as a dessert.

Store well wrapped in an airtight tin. Do not refrigerate.

Baking

Lemon Yoghurt Cake

Chocolate Fridge Cake

A no-bake treat that's easy to make with children. As long as you use the quantities listed, you can 'pick 'n' mix' the filling ingredients to suit your taste and mood.

Makes 12 squares.

Ingredients

250g digestive biscuits
300g dark chocolate
100g butter
100g golden syrup

50g dried apricots finely chopped
50g dried cranberries
75g raisins
30g mixed nuts (optional)

Method

Crush the biscuits. I do this with a rolling pin so I get a mixture of sizes to the crumb and I enjoy the bashing!

Next, melt the butter with the chocolate and syrup in a heat proof bowl over barely simmering water. Don't allow the bowl to touch the water, and don't let the water boil.

Once melted, add the remaining ingredients, stir to mix.

Firm into a 20cm square tin and refrigerate until set.

Cut into squares and store in the fridge in an airtight container.

Acknowledgements and Thanks

This book wouldn't have been possible without the hard work and dedication of my husband, Tony Ross. Not only did he try most of the recipes - multiple times - he also painstakingly designed the entire book from cover to cover, proof-read it and produced the print-ready PDF's. His support for the project, and for me, has been nothing short of amazing.

Huge thanks must also go to my beta-testers - Chris Carini, Lynn Cole, Paula Harmon, Michael Gallacher, Helen Sedgwick, Julia Smith and Tracy Stickler - without whom my daft mistakes would never have been picked up, and whose valuable feedback improved the readability of the recipes no end. Your time and effort in cooking dishes and offering feedback has been essential to producing a cookbook I can be proud of.

Shout out to friends and family who have been full of support and encouragement for this project. It means a lot.

Thanks also to Stuart Clifford for my wooden chopping board; star of many a photo shoot.

Thanks are also due to Hazel and Iain at Thomson's, who were patient and helpful throughout the printing process, and to Sue Lawrence, who readily and generously agreed to look at the text and give her comments.

Last, but by no means least, thanks to Chris Asher and Sheenagh Harrison for the loan of their lovely crockery - antique plates, hand-painted bowls and Wedgewood - which provided for some variety and colour to display the dishes in this book.

Index

Index (continued)

cooking notes

cooking notes